PLATO'S
THE REPUBLIC

A BEGINNER'S GUIDE

HARRY EYRES

Hodder & Stoughton

A MEMBER OF THE HODDER HEADLINE GROUP

For Irene, an always encouraging friend,
to whom Plato means so much.

Orders: please contact Bookpoint Ltd, 130 Milton Park, Abingdon, Oxon OX14 4TD. Telephone:
(44) 01235 827720, Fax: (44) 01235 400454. Lines are open from 9.00–6.00, Monday to Saturday,
with a 24-hour message answering service. Email address: orders@bookpoint.co.uk

British Library Cataloguing in Publication Data
A catalogue record for this title is available from The British Library

ISBN 0 340 80420 3

First published 2001
Impression number   10 9 8 7 6 5 4 3 2 1
Year 2007 2006 2005 2004 2003 2002

Cover photo from Corbis Images.
Typeset by Transet Limited, Coventry, England.
Printed in Great Britain for Hodder & Stoughton Educational, a division of Hodder Headline
Plc, 338 Euston Road, London NW1 3BH by Cox & Wyman, Reading, Berks.

CONTENTS

ACKNOWLEDGEMENT

W. B. Yeats: extract from 'A Dialogue of Self and Soul' from *Collected Poems*, reprinted by permission of A. P. Watt Ltd. on behalf of Michael B. Yeats.

FOREWORD

Welcome to ...

Hodder & Stoughton's Beginner's Guides to Great Works

... your window into the world of the big ideas!

This series brings home for you the classics of western and world thought. These are the guides to the books everyone wants to have read – the greatest moments in science and philosophy, theology and psychology, politics and history. Even in the age of the Internet, these are the books that keep their lasting appeal. As so much becomes ephemeral – the text message, the e-mail, the season's hit that is forgotten in a few weeks – we have a deeper need of something more lasting. These are the books that connect the ages, shining the light of the past on the changing present, and expanding the horizons of the future.

However, the great works are not always the most immediately accessible. Though they speak to us directly, in flashes, they are also expressions of human experience and perceptions at its most complex. The purpose of these guides is to take you into the world of these books, so that they can speak directly to your experience.

WHAT COUNTS AS A GREAT WORK?

There is no fixed list of great works. Our aim is to offer as comprehensive and varied a selection as possible from among the books which include:

* **The key points of influence** on science, ethics, religious beliefs, political values, psychological understanding.

* The finest achievements of **the greatest authors**.

* The origins and climaxes in **the great movements** of thought and belief.

* The most provocative arguments, which have aroused **the strongest reactions**, including the most notorious as well as the most praised works.

* The high points of **intellectual style**, wit and persuasion.

READING THIS GUIDE

There are many ways to enjoy this book – whether you are thinking of reading the great work, or have tried and want some support, or have enjoyed it and want some help to clarify and express your reactions.

These guides will help you appreciate your chosen book if you are taking a course, or if you are following your own pathway.

What this guide offers

Each guide aims:

* To tell the whole story of the book, from its origins to its influence.

* To follow the book's argument in a careful and lively way.

* To explain the key terms and concepts.

* To bring in accessible examples.

* To provide further reading and wider questions to explore.

How to approach this guide

These guides are designed to be a coherent read, keeping you turning the pages from start to finish – maybe even in a sitting or two!

At the same time, the guide is also a reference work that you can consult repeatedly as you read the great work or after finishing a passage. To make both reading and consulting easy, the guides have:

* Boxes identifying where we are in the reading of the great work.

* Key quotations with page references to different editions.

* Explanations of key quotes.

Our everyday life is buzzing with messages that get shorter and more disposable every month. Through this guide, you can enter a more lasting dialogue of ideas.

George Myerson, Series Editor

A NOTE ABOUT QUOTATIONS AND TRANSLATIONS

Quotations are taken from the translation by J. L. Davies and D. J. Vaughan, London: Macmillan (1885). The number references in the text are the page numbers from Volume II of the Greek edition of *The Republic* by H. Stephaunus (Paris, 1578). These numbers appear in the margins of all subsequent editions and translations of *The Republic*.

There are readable modern translations by H. D. P. Lee (Harmondsworth: Penguin Classics, 1955) and Allan Bloom (Basic Books, 1991).

MAIN CHARACTERS OF THE DIALOGUE

Socrates

Glaucon, a young man, brother of Plato

Adeimantus, a young man, brother of Plato

Polemarchus, a young man

Cephalus, a wealthy old man, father of Polemarchus

Thrasymachus, a Sophist

Minor characters:
Lysias and Euthydemus (brothers of Polemarchus), Charmantides and Cleitophon.

A GREAT WORK: PLATO'S *THE REPUBLIC*

The Republic, written probably in the 380s BC, is the longest, most wide-ranging and most influential of all Plato's Socratic dialogues. Fired by the desire to track down justice, the conversation between Socrates and his interlocutors turns into a great and all-embracing philosophical journey. *The Republic:*

* covers an astonishing range of topics, from education, art, politics and psychology through equality of the sexes to the nature of philosophy itself and its ultimate goal, the good.

* is the most ambitious single-volume attempt in the whole of Western philosophy to establish guiding principles of human conduct, both individual and collective.

* has had an unparalleled influence on subsequent thinkers and practitioners in the areas of political science, educational theory, psychology, metaphysics, ethics, theology and the theory of art.

PLATO'S *THE REPUBLIC*: SPECIAL FEATURES

This Beginner's Guide aims to bring to life the reading of this great work, and to put that reading in context. *The Republic* is written as a seamless, conversational whole, and the Guide tries to retain the sense of freewheeling flow, while pausing sufficiently to explain and carefully consider key passages, ideas, and words.

Key Quotation Boxes: these highlight extracts which are central to the understanding of Plato's argument.

Quotation Boxes: these frame especially eloquent and memorable passages from the original text which are woven into the guided reading.

Key Argument and Concept Boxes: these shaded boxes present concise summaries of Plato's main arguments and concepts.

Keyword Boxes: these shaded boxes explain the most important words from the original text, whose range of meanings in Greek is often hard to convey precisely in English translation.

Other boxes conveniently gather together important background and context materials.

INTRODUCTION: THE CAVE

At the heart of Plato's *Republic* is one of the most disturbing and fertile images in world literature. The dialogue's main speaker, Socrates, compares human beings to prisoners in a cave. They are fettered by their necks and legs, so they can look only at what is in front of them; they spend their time watching shadows projected on a wall facing them, cast by images passed along a road in front of a fire and accompanied by sound effects. Because they can see neither their own situation nor how the shadows and sound-effects are created, they mistake them for real people and objects.

At this point Socrates imagines one of the prisoners being somehow released from her fetters and first made to stand up and face the fire, before being led up the difficult ascent out of the Cave and into the sunlight. There is a double difficulty of adjustment of vision; first the released prisoner finds the daylight too bright and is dazzled. Then, having got used to the light of reality and to seeing things as they are, the released prisoner is reluctant to go back down into the Cave. When she does so (as the good of the community as a whole demands) she has trouble becoming rehabituated to the darkness of the shadow-world, unlike the 'experts' among the prisoners who are particularly good at interpreting the meaning of the shadow-play. Her task is to lead the other prisoners to 'see the light', but it will not be an easy one, and may be dangerous or even fatal.

This extraordinary 'myth', which has exercised many of the greatest thinkers of the West, from Aristotle to Augustine, Bacon and Jung, distils much of the long, complex argument of *The Republic*. Immediately striking is that this is a dramatic image of the human predicament, not a piece of abstract philosophizing. Here, in the most charged passage of his greatest book, Plato proceeds not from disinterested logical intelligence but from concern for how human beings live. Before we are invited to 'see' the image – and despite the fact that seeing remains the dominant metaphor for knowledge in

The Republic – we are told that what is to follow concerns *what human beings go through*. The Greek word here is *pathos*, experience or suffering.

The Cave myth presents the plight of humanity – and a pretty dire plight it is. Human beings are unfree (surely Rousseau had the Cave in mind when he wrote 'Man is born free, and everywhere he is in chains,' and Marx and Engels when they proclaimed 'The proletarians have nothing to lose but their chains'); but even more disastrously, they are unaware of their unfreedom. The key to this lack of freedom – which is both political and psychological – is that human beings are profoundly removed from reality. They live in the semi-darkness of an underground cavern (though not completely sealed off from sunlight). Not only that, but they have become habituated to this benighted environment. The play of shadows on the wall is clearly, to use a modern-sounding word, entertaining. The Cave is rather like a cinema, and the myth seems an uncannily accurate premonition of the contemporary world's fascination with moving images on screens.

In Plato's view, people are 'turned the wrong way round'. They are locked in a rigid and erroneous mind-set, entranced by a passing show of insubstantial unrealities. Here he has in mind such things as power, status, sex, superficial cleverness, plausibility. The obsession with such attractive but unfulfilling objects is not only lamentable but dangerous. It leads to chaos both at the individual and social level. This is the true source of the political disasters which continue to afflict the world (and our world does not seem less afflicted in this regard than Plato's). The task, which is the true theme of *The Republic*, is to 'convert' people, to turn them round so they can see how things really are. How is this task – surely an educational or therapeutic task before it is a political one – to be accomplished? The long, labyrinthine argument of *The Republic* is an attempt to find the answer.

APPROACHING *THE REPUBLIC*

Approaching *The Republic* – a long philosophical work written nearly 2400 years ago in a now dead language – might seem a daunting business. However, *The Republic* is infinitely more readable than nearly all the great philosophical works which have succeeded it (apart from those of Montaigne, Nietzsche and one or two others). Anyone expecting a dry treatise may be delighted to come across a work of remarkable liveliness, full of humour and dramatic touches – and marked by passages which combine elevated thought, passionate feeling and poetic intensity in a way hardly matched in world literature. *The Republic*, as well as a great book of philosophy, is an extraordinary work of art which manages to convey the sense of an ongoing, freewheeling conversation for more than 300 pages.

The difficulty of *The Republic* is not so much a technical difficulty (though there are some tricky passages) as something more subtle. At 432 Socrates says:

> QUOTATION
> *We must be like hunters surrounding a cover and must give close attention that justice may nowhere escape us and disappear from our view.*

What he says about justice, the ostensible theme of *The Republic*, could be applied to the dialogue itself. What kind of animal is *The Republic*? Rather a slippery and elusive one, it seems, whose true nature may well have escaped most of the learned minds who have tried to grasp it over the centuries. And before we try to answer that question, here are some other, equally important ones. What is *The Republic* really about – what is its main theme? Is *The Republic* a political blueprint? What is its relationship to practicability and feasibility? How serious is *The Republic*, or how seriously are we meant to take it?

How serious is *The Republic*?

Let us look at that last question first. It might seem self-evident that *The Republic* is a pretty serious book – certainly Plato's most ambitious and comprehensive attempt to 'follow to its source/ Every event in action or in thought' as the poet W. B. Yeats put it (in 'A Dialogue of Self and Soul' from *Collected Poems*, Lonson: MacMillan, 1950, p.267). Some commentators have certainly taken it in deadly earnest, concluding that its author is little or no better than a fascist dictator. But *The Republic* hardly reads like a text by Mussolini, Hitler or Stalin. It is not only cast in the form of a conversation – Plato says nothing in *The Republic* – but its tone is conversational, subtle, ironic. For some commentators irony is the key to reading *The Republic* (see the discussion in Chapter 1).

Time and time again, the text warns the reader not to take it too seriously. At 536, Socrates remarks: '*I forgot... that we were not serious, and spoke too earnestly.*' Almost sheepishly at 473, on the point of making the key statement of the entire dialogue (that unless philosophers rule in the city or those currently called rulers apply themselves diligently to philosophy, there will be no end to human troubles), Socrates admits to his young interlocutor Glaucon that he expects to be '*deluge[d] with laughter and infamy.*' Glaucon duly obliges.

Laughter comes up frequently in *The Republic*. There is even an idea that there might be something faintly ridiculous about the whole 'thing', the 'edifice' constructed out of (written) words. Words written, but made to appear spoken. Here we might look forward to what is said by Socrates about writing in a later dialogue, the *Phaedrus:*

> *He who thinks that anything in writing will be clear and certain, would be an utterly simple person... you might think [written words] spoke as if they had intelligence, but if you question them, wishing to know about their saying, they always say only one and*

the same thing... is there not another kind of word... the word which is written with intelligence in the mind of the learner, which is able to defend itself and knows to whom it should speak, and before whom to be silent?

(*Phaedrus* 275–6)

Here Socrates seems to be implying that there is something dumb, even ridiculous about written texts (or most written texts), which are not open to the lively interplay of conversation, which go on repeating the same thing like records stuck in a groove.

Socrates himself did not write anything – but his disparagement of writing (which has been challenged by Jacques Derrida, especially in the essay 'Plato's Pharmacy' in *Dissemination*, London: Athlone Press, 1981) is given to us by Plato in written form, though in a kind of writing which simulates conversation. Just before this, at *Phaedrus* 265, Socrates says, apropos of the rather astonishing conversation he has just had with Phaedrus, '*the discourse was, as a whole, really sportive jest.*' The word to play (*paizein*) comes up frequently in *The Republic*, for example at 537 where Socrates says '*you must train the children... in a playful manner, and without any air of constraint.*'

The lesson to be drawn from this concerns the spirit in which we approach *The Republic*. Any approach which is too serious or humourless or utterly unplayful surely goes against the spirit of the text. For all its length and complexity, there is something light and airy about *The Republic*. It is perhaps the original castle in the air. Key to understanding the nature of the 'construction' are the Greek words *oikizeim* and *oikein* which are used repeatedly to describe what is going on in *The Republic* (for example, 420). *Oikizein* can mean both to build a house and to found a settlement; *oikein* to inhabit, to settle and to govern. Socrates talks about the business of *The Republic* as '*oikizein polin*', founding the city. However, Plato obviously wants to found something more or other than the city: *The Republic*, with breathtaking ambition, will attempt to establish firm unshakeable principles not just of politics but also of education, psychology, art and ultimately of epistemology (how we know things) and ontology (the nature of reality). But the building material of the dialogue, as Socrates often stresses, consists of words. Near the end at 592 Glaucon speaks of '*the city whose organisation we have now completed, and which is confined to the region of speculation*,' and continues: '*I do not believe it is to be found anywhere on earth.*' Socrates, who earlier has insisted that the well-governed society is a possibility, seems ruefully to agree:

QUOTATION

Perhaps in heaven there is laid up a pattern of it for him who wishes to behold it, and beholding, to organise himself accordingly.

Is *The Republic* a political blueprint?

It is perhaps too simple to say that *The Republic* is not and never was a political blueprint – a feasible plan for a well-governed society. An ambivalence runs through the dialogue (as it does through Plato's life). On the one hand, thought must be allowed to run free, not to concern itself with the immediate practicability of proposals; but on the other, there is the recognition that if there is ever to be an end to human suffering and chaos, there must be radical reform, or reformation, in practice and not just in theory. Plato's concern with politics took a practical, serious and ultimately disastrous turn in his extended relations with Dionysius I and II, tyrants of Sicily, and the former's brother-in-law Dion. His last work, *The Laws*, returns to the theme of founding a well-governed society, this time in considerably more detail (but without the dream of philosopher-kings).

All the same, *The Republic* is more of an educational and therapeutic 'thought-adventure' than a blueprint. It is an adventure in thinking things, or human affairs, through, starting with what seems the most important, justice. *The Republic* will teach us how to think, so that both individually and collectively we may lead better, more 'upright' lives. If this sounds archaic, simplistic or moralistic, it is also remarkably modern. Despite Nietzsche's antipathy to Socrates and Plato, *The Republic* anticipates Nietzsche's project of therapeutic philosophy. If Plato stands at the head of the tradition of academic philosophy, he is also the origin of the very different tradition of philosophy as therapy which was dominant in the Hellenistic world and in which the modern disciplines or practices of psychoanalysis and psychotherapy can be located.

It is in the nature of an adventure that unexpected things will happen along the way – indeed that the way is not mapped out in advance. *The Republic* only really finds itself when it tackles the question of philosophy and what it is to be a philosopher in Book 6. One idea is constantly leading to another in *The Republic*. The main themes, justice, education, politics, psychology, philosophy, poetry are not dealt with in neat chunks but keep reappearing and being developed and transformed throughout the dialogue. The effect is that both interlocutors and readers discover the interconnectedness of things. Politics cannot really be separated from psychology; the just society cannot be considered apart from the upright individual; a political system depends on an educational system; you cannot reform the state without radically rethinking the family; educational, political, psychological questions are bound up with theories of knowledge and reality and of art and representation. The questions just keep coming in *The Republic* . It is characterized not by a systematic neatness but by a determination to tackle every question, to challenge every authority and to trace everything back to its source. In this sense, despite its frequent bouts of authoritarianism, *The Republic* is one of the most radical books ever written.

1 Plato and Socrates in their worlds

Who were Plato and Socrates and what was the relationship between them? The two men were both citizens of Athens, which for a while during the latter part of the fifth century BC became the most powerful city-state in Greece, before it was defeated by Sparta in the long Peloponnesian War. Politically, Athens stood for democracy and under the city's unique democratic system, all male citizens (except for slaves) took an active part in governing. This gave it great advantages (though Plato did not see it this way) over its rivals. Athens not only grew rich and powerful as a dynamic trading centre, and ultimately imperial power, but also became the acknowledged cultural centre of the Greek world. Under Pericles, the city was adorned with splendid buildings. The most spectacular, those of the Acropolis (the rock-fortress which dominates Athens), including the Parthenon and the Erechtheion, though partly ruined, still stand magnificently over the modern metropolis of Athens. Athens was also the Greek centre for drama: it was to the city's Dionysia festival that aspiring playwrights from all over Greece came hoping to win prizes. The three most famous tragedians – Aeschylus, Sophocles and Euripides – and the comedian Aristophanes were widely celebrated in their time and continue to be performed and admired today.

In terms of what came to be defined as philosophy (by Plato), Athens had not been the Greek centre before Socrates's time. The thinkers now known as the Presocratics, who combined metaphysical inquiry with scientific-type investigation, including Thales, Democritus, Heraclitus, Anaximander and Anaxagoras, mainly came from Ionia (the modern-day west coast of Turkey). The last of these came to Athens in around 460 BC and became a friend of Pericles. His view that the universe is governed by a force he called

Nous (intelligence or spirit) impressed Socrates (see below) and had a far-reaching influence on all later Greek and Western thought.

In the famous autobiographical passage of the *Phaedo* Socrates relates how he became dissatisfied with the kind of scientific thinking which assigned material causes to things. Anaxagoras's Nous promised a way out of this cul-de-sac but soon disappointed Socrates because it incorporated no rationale of 'what is best'. The Socratic turn is away from investigation of natural phenomena and towards inquiry into the nature and relationship of goodness and knowledge.

WHO WAS SOCRATES?

Socrates was born around 469 BC into a modest family. His father is said to have been a sculptor and his mother a midwife. He played no very prominent part in the city's affairs until middle age. Around 430 BC the Delphic Oracle (the most respected religious authority in Greece, though often suspected of deviousness in secular affairs) declared that Socrates was the wisest man in Athens. From this moment on Socrates was engaged on his mission: first to disprove the oracle, then, when he found that it was true in the limited sense that he was the only person aware of his own lack of wisdom, to cross-question fellow citizens about issues of morality, education, knowledge and skill. In 423 BC Aristophanes portrayed Socrates in his comedy *The Clouds* as the archetypal 'nutty professor,' who runs a thinking-shop called the Phrontisterion and is dedicated to apparently pointless scientific questions and to disproving the tenets of common sense. Socrates was an obvious choice for satirical portraiture, not just because of his unconventional ideas but also because of his famously unprepossessing appearance: bald head, snub nose, beetling brows and infrequently washed cloak.

More seriously, a number of Socrates's pupils (he claimed not to be a teacher in the conventional sense but many young men were drawn to his ambit) became involved with the aristocratic counter-movement to Athenian democracy which culminated in the putsch of 404 BC led by one of Socrates's closest associates, Critias. This coincided with the final defeat of Athens in the Peloponnesian War with Sparta.

In 399 BC there occurred one of the most famous trials in history. Socrates was accused of introducing new gods and of corrupting the youth of Athens, though it has always been assumed that the motive for his impeachment was primarily political. His speech in his own defence is recorded (no doubt elaborated) in Plato's *The Apology*, and his final hours, after he has been found guilty and condemned to death, in the *Phaedo*. Both in *The Apology* and the *Phaedo* Socrates refers to his family: his wife's name was Xanthippe and his sons were still young at the time of his death. In *The Apology* Socrates says, *'I have been literally attached by God to our city, as though it were a large thorough-bred horse which because of its great size is inclined to be lazy and needs the stimulation of a gadfly.'* Socrates's dignified death (the method of execution was poisoning by hemlock) is described in the closing words of the *Phaedo*:

> *Such was the end, Echecrates, of our friend, who was, as we may say, of all those of his time whom we have known, the best and wisest and most upright man.*

Socratic sayings

'The unexamined life is not worth living.' (*The Apology*)

'It is never right to do wrong or to requite wrong with wrong, or when we suffer evil defend ourselves by doing evil in return.' (*Crito*)

'And I tell you that virtue does not come from money, but from virtue come money and all the other good things to man, both to the individual and to the state.' (*The Apology*)

WHO WAS PLATO?

Socrates's most devoted and brilliant disciple, Plato, came from a background very different from his mentor's. He was born around 429 BC into an aristocratic family (Plato is, in fact, a nickname meaning 'broad-shouldered') and must have got to know Socrates as a very young man. Socrates's teachings had an immense effect on Plato: Socrates appears as the main speaker in nearly all Plato's dialogues and Plato's long life-work is an attempt to expound and complete the philosophy of the man he regarded as his own teacher and the exemplary philosopher and human being. Plato's philosophy ultimately rests on the fact that a man once existed who was truly good, who challenged prevailing ideas of goodness and knowledge using a particular method of conversational cross-examination.

PLATO'S INVOLVEMENT WITH POLITICS

In the autobiographical *Seventh Letter*, the authenticity of which is disputed, Plato talks about his early (and later) involvement with politics, before his eventual and rueful decision to abandon practical statesmanship in favour of teaching and philosophy. He describes how, as a very young man, he was drawn to take part for a short time in the oligarchic regime of the Thirty, which took power in Athens in 404 BC, before withdrawing in disgust when the Thirty attempted to force Socrates to take part in the arrest of an innocent man. He recognized that the restored democracy was in most ways preferable, though under it Socrates was condemned to death. This event seems to have coloured all Plato's later thinking and casts a long shadow over *The Republic.* In the 390s BC Plato travelled quite extensively, but his conclusion was that '*all existing societies were badly governed.*' In 387 BC he returned to Athens and founded the Academy in an olive grove outside the city walls of Athens as 'a combination of a school and institute of scientific research' (R. Crossman, *Plato Today*, p.77).

The most dramatic and controversial episodes in Plato's life were his three visits to the Sicilian city-state of Syracuse, then the largest in the Greek world. The first visit occurred around 389 BC and Plato was not impressed by the debauchery of the Syracusan Court or the ruler Dionysius I. This ruthless real-politician is probably the model for the memorable portrait of the tyrant in *The Republic* Book 9. However, on this first visit Plato met Dionysius's brother-in-law Dion, who was to become a close friend and the most important influence on Plato after Socrates. It was Dion who persuaded Plato to return to Syracuse in 367 BC when Dionysius I died and was succeeded by his son Dionysius II, with Dion as the éminence grise behind the throne. The idea was that Plato – who by this time had written *The Republic* – should supervise young Dionysius's education and advise him on policy. Here, Plato must have thought, was a possible 'philosopher-king.'

The historian Plutarch reports the enthusiasm with which Plato was greeted and the auspicious beginning of his mission. Riotous excesses were curbed, and still more amazingly, '*there was a general passion for reasoning and philosophy.*' This state of affairs could not last. Dionysius became impatient with his abstract studies (perhaps based on the curriculum of *The Republic* Book 7); the influence of Plato and Dion was resented, and a battle for power ensued between Dion and the general Philistos. Dion was banished and shortly afterwards Plato returned to Athens, though with an invitation to return.

Plato's third and final visit in 361 BC was nearly disastrous. A serious quarrel had developed between Dionysius and Dion and Plato was summoned, in effect, as mediator. He became a virtual prisoner of Dionysius, who had confiscated Dion's property and proceeded to sell it off. Having narrowly escaped death during a mutiny, Plato managed to get away in a boat sent by his friend Archytas of Tarentum. In 357 BC Dion invited Plato to join him in an expedition to capture Syracuse. Plato refused. The expedition went ahead; Dion captured the city and set up an authoritarian regime on Platonic lines. The results were dismal; civil war broke out and Dion eventually had his chief rival Heracleides murdered. In 353 BC Dion, in turn, was murdered by Kallippus, a former student at Plato's Academy.

What does Plato's involvement with Syracusan politics tell us about him and his great work, *The Republic*? First of all, Plato was unable to resist an opportunity to exercise an active or even decisive influence on the governance of a powerful city-state. This rather belies the idea that Plato was interested only in theoretical 'city-building'. However, the way things turned out surely even more decisively disproves the idea of Plato as a totalitarian political programmer, or even a 'fascist'. His main influence, such as it was, seems to have been moral and educational. The great philosopher was clearly both repelled and out of depth when a real power struggle broke out in Syracuse. More serious is the charge that his ideas encouraged the ill-fated political experiments of Dion. Dion may have been misled by certain rather casual references to the use of force in *The Republic* to misread that text as sanctioning political brutality, whereas its main thrust is unmistakably towards the making of a moral individual.

THE PLATO/SOCRATES RELATIONSHIP

Plato and Socrates were in many ways opposites. Socrates, even though he eventually came to grief there, seems to have been entirely at home in Athens, cheerfully traipsing the streets, talking to all and sundry. Plato (who never married) comes across as a more aloof figure, who did not suffer fools gladly. Socrates's whole attitude was unprofessional: he claimed not to be a teacher and received no money from teaching. Plato, by contrast, set up the Academy, perhaps the world's first university. Above all, Socrates is the great conversationalist and Plato the great writer.

Of course, all this presupposes that we know where Socrates ends and Plato begins. Most of the important thoughts in Plato's dialogues are spoken by Socrates, or rather the character Socrates. It would be naive to assume that Plato's character Socrates is identical to the historical Socrates. Although, through the many dialogues, Plato's portrait has come to dominate perceptions of Socrates, especially in the last 200 years, there is a rival portrait in Xenophon's *Memorabilia*. For centuries this exercised an equal or greater influence on people's ideas of who Socrates was. Readers may have felt they were getting a 'straighter' version of Socrates from Xenophon who, to say the least, is a much plainer writer than Plato, lacking philosophical depth and poetic intensity. Xenophon's Socrates comes across as garrulous, pious and sententious, a doler out of homilies. Kierkegaard could not understand how the Athenians could have decided that such a man deserved to be put to death.

PLATO'S SOCRATIC DIALOGUES
The Platonic Socrates is not only a more mysterious and challenging figure, he also changes quite radically through the dialogues. These dialogues can be split into three:

Early dialogues
Plato's early dialogues are often called 'aporetic' (from the Greek word *aporia*, meaning a place of puzzlement and perplexity). In these Socrates does not speak at great length as he does in *The Republic*, but cross-questions others (the Greek word for this cross-examination is *elenchus*), getting them to reveal the inconsistencies in their initial positions. He shows that prevailing definitions of virtues or qualities such as courage (*Laches*), friendship (*Hippias Minor*), poetry (*Ion*) are unsatisfactory, without putting forward positive definitions of his own.

Middle dialogues
The 'middle period' dialogues include Plato's most famous works: *The Apology, Phaedo, Meno, The Republic, The Symposium, Phaedrus.* These develop Plato's own thinking (expressed through the voice of Socrates) on the nature of the soul (*Phaedo* and *Phaedrus*), love (*The Symposium* and *Phaedrus*), goodness, justice, wisdom and knowledge (*The Republic*).

Late dialogues

In the 'late period' dialogues Plato continues to investigate questions of wisdom and knowledge, goodness (*Philebus*), political justice (*Statesman*) and the relation of all these to ultimate and unchanging reality. The *Timaeus*, hugely influential in later antiquity, offers a mathematically based cosmology. His last and longest work, *The Laws* from which Socrates is absent, gives a much more elaborate and practical account of an 'ideal state' than the inspired sketch of *The Republic*.

SOCRATIC AND PLATONIC IRONY

Socrates was not only famed as an ironic individual, he more or less invented irony. Before Socrates, the Greek word *eiron* meant little more than 'a cunning deceiver'. Plato's Socrates inaugurated irony as one of the most important and complex of literary devices. Several times in Plato's works Socrates is described as *eironeumenos*, practising irony. When the sophist Thrasymachus confronts him in *The Republic* Book I, he knows he is going to be subjected to Socrates's famous irony. In *The Symposium* Socrates is described as '*spending his life playfully practising irony towards his fellow men.*' Socrates's reputation as an ironist, as Alexander Nehamas shows in *The Art of Living* (1998), is confirmed by the later classical writers Aristotle, Cicero and Quintilian. In the *Nicomachean Ethics* Aristotle identifies Socrates as an ironist, and contrasts ironists, '*who understate things...[and] speak not for gain but to avoid parade,*' with boasters. Cicero, in *De Oratore*, speaks of the '*dissimulation when the things said are different from what you understand... In this irony and dissimulation Socrates, in my opinion, far excelled all others in charm and humanity.*' Quintilian, in *Institutio Oratoria*, goes the furthest of all in identifying Socrates with irony when he writes, '*an entire life can be seen to be characterised by irony, as we see in the case of Socrates.*'

But what exactly is Socratic irony? Alexander Nehamas gives a beautifully subtle account in *The Art of Living* and argues that it is nothing so simple as saying the opposite of what you mean. Rather, it is a distancing device, dissociating the speaker from what he says. You could also say that Socratic irony is above all a particular tone. If you were on the wrong end of it you might well feel tricked, but Socrates's intention is not merely to make a fool of others, but to introduce a note of radical uncertainty, which applies to what he says as much as to what others say.

There is also the question of Platonic irony. By the time *The Republic* was written, Socrates had become more the philosophical voice of Plato than he was in the earlier dialogues. Socratic irony is still present, as a playful tone which often disclaims knowledge, but its role is less important. Plato's irony, Nehamas argues, is directed towards the reader. We should beware of any position of false superiority, of believing that we know better than the hapless interlocutors Polemarchus, Glaucon and Adeimantus, or Thrasymachus. We may still be in the Cave without knowing it. A young contemporary writer, author of a work on the cultural imperialism of big corporations and their brands, criticizes her contemporaries for being too preoccupied with '*the politics of image, not action*,' and in so doing evokes Plato's Cave: '*We were too busy analysing the pictures on the wall to notice that the wall itself had been sold*' (Naomi Klein, *No Logo*, London: Flamingo, 2000, p.124).

Towards justice

The Republic opens with the casual, informal air of someone talking about something which just happened to happen to them the day before:

> QUOTATION
> *I went down yesterday to the Piraeus with Glaucon the son of Ariston.*

There is no indication that the reader is about to embark on a great philosophical journey. The walk to the port of Piraeus from Athens is not particularly long. Philosophical discussion is not Socrates's purpose: he has gone down to the Piraeus to say a prayer and to take a look at a festival being celebrated there. Socrates and Glaucon are on their way home when a slave sent by Polemarchus grabs Socrates's coat. He will not be allowed to get away; the future of *The Republic* hangs on the length of a piece of cloth. In this artful opening Socrates is established as the ultimately mysterious character whose purposes are never disclosed, someone who is not a professional teacher or philosopher, but around whom teaching or philosophy happens. The context and impetus for that philosophy is the eager enthusiasm of young men who want to ask questions.

It's playful stuff, with an erotic tinge. Adeimantus (like Glaucon, a brother of Plato) promises horse-racing, Polemarchus adds a carnival and above all '*many young men with whom we can converse*'. Perhaps this is directed primarily at the young Glaucon, but Socrates does not demur at his young friend's willingness to be detained. Soon Socrates finds himself in conversation with Polemarchus's father, old Cephalus. The conversation starts off on the theme of old age and then moves through sexual love to wealth. Cephalus is a rich man and Socrates questions him about the advantages of being rich. Now something important happens. Cephalus says that the main advantage of being rich is in helping a man to avoid wrong-doing. In fact there is a sudden spate of words denoting doing right and wrong, the words from the Greek root *dike*. Suddenly Socrates's ears seem to prick up: something important is at stake here, the nature of 'doing right', or 'justice' – the Greek *dikaiosyne*. Socrates is hooked, the dialogue has found its theme and is on its way.

> **KEYWORD**
>
> The Greek words *dikaios* and *dikaiosyne* are normally translated as 'just' and 'justice'. But they cover a wider spectrum of meanings than any equivalent words in English, from social justice to individual righteousness. The meanings of *dikaios* range from 'lawful' to 'upright', 'righteous' and even 'good'.

What follows, first with Cephalus, then with Polemarchus and Thraysmachus, is a characteristic piece of Socratic *elenchus*, questioning and examination. This part of *The Republic*, untypically, harks back to the earlier aporetic dialogues. Socrates is not at all satisfied with Cephalus's definition of 'doing right' as avoiding lying and paying one's debts. But the old man doesn't really have the appetite for this sort of discussion (it might raise inconvenient questions). He goes off to the sacrifice, leaving the philosophizing to the younger men.

POLEMARCHUS AND CONVENTIONAL IDEAS OF JUSTICE

The main purpose of the discussion of justice between Socrates and Polemarchus, and then the dramatic 'duel' of words between Socrates and the Sophist Thrasymachus, is to flush out both unthinkingly conventional and fashionably cynical ideas of justice and expose them as unsatisfactory. Polemarchus is very convenient here because he thinks in conventional terms. He comes up with the definition, sanctioned by the poet Simonides, '*to restore to each man what is his due, is just*' and the notion that justice is useful in money matters. Socrates's method is *reductio ad absurdum*. In the first case you get the result, at 332, '*justice... means doing good to our friends and harm to our enemies*' (not immediately absurd but obviously not Socrates's view) and in the second, at 334, that '*the just man is a kind of thief*' (because those who are good at keeping money will also be good at stealing it!).

KEY ARGUMENT

Polemarchus's definitions are all really based in self-interest. He can't distinguish between a legalistic definition of justice and an ethical one.

All this seems rather nit-picking and unsatisfactory, but there are bigger issues at stake. Socrates obviously has a much higher, more wide-reaching sense of justice even if it can't be fully articulated yet. He wonders first whether justice is a kind of skill or art (*techne*), then discerns that its role is more sweeping: something to do with goodness, and the common good of all, knowledge. '*Justice is a human excellence*' (335); doing right must involve knowing what you are doing; goodness can never have anything to do with harming people. But to get to the bottom of those suggestive ideas will take the best part of 300 pages of fathoming.

THE DUEL WITH THRASYMACHUS: SOCRATIC VERSUS SOPHISTIC APPROACHES

At this point the vulnerable, newly hatched justice is suddenly subjected to a frontal assault. The entry into the discussion of Thrasymachus ('*like a wild beast*') is the most dramatic moment in the entire dialogue. His duel with Socrates works on at least two levels. On one level it is a debate about justice and injustice, and which 'pays' better. On another level it works as an exemplary contrast of two styles of argumentation and teaching, the **Sophistic** and the **Socratic**. In fact, it's the contrast in styles which is highlighted first. Thrasymachus has no truck with Socratic irony, which he sees both as an easy way out ('*it is easier to ask questions than to answer them*' – 336) and as a sham, a pretence of ignorance.

Thrasymachus changes the whole course of the argument, and of *The Republic*, by bringing politics into the discussion. Though apparently an outsider, he represents the voice of the city. His first main contention is that justice is merely whatever is in the interests of the stronger party – or the government. You could call this the might is right argument. A very modern-seeming corollary to this is relativism: justice will change according to the nature of the regime in power: democratic states will make democratic laws, tyrannical regimes tyrannical ones and so on.

> **KEYWORD**
>
> **The Sophists:** Thrasymachus is a typical Sophist. The Sophists were the Western world's first professional intellectuals, who appeared in the fifth century BC as itinerant teachers who challenged prevailing ideas and taught intellectual skills. Plato obviously despised them both for their shallowly relativistic ideas and their corruption of true teaching into a kind of intellectual prostitution.

Thrasymachus' argument should seem contemporary to British readers: the Scott Report into arms for Iraq showed that British government ministers in the late 1980s and early 1990s repeatedly made no distinction between public interest and government interest. They were prepared to use so-called Public Interest Immunity Certificates to protect the government and allow innocent men to face wrongful imprisonment.

Socrates's riposte seems at best technical, at worst tricksy. Socrates asks if rulers always know what is in their interest. If they are sometimes mistaken (as Thrasymachus has to concede), then in those cases even according to Thrasymachus's argument it would be right for their subjects to disobey them. The argument at this point verges on the absurd – more like a wrestling bout than a genuine debate. But Socrates does have a serious point, which has huge repercussions for *The Republic*, and for later political thinking: it is that governing or ruling is a specific skill, like medicine or ship-captaincy. Skills by definition are exercised not for self-interest but in the interest of the subject (the point of medicine is to cure the patient not the doctor). Socrates's conclusion here is important:

> ## KEY QUOTATION
> *And thus, Thrasymachus, all who are in any place of command, in so far as they are rulers, neither consider nor enjoin their own interest, but that of the subjects for whom they exercise their craft: and in all that they do or say, they act with an exclusive view to them, and to what is good and proper for them.* (342)

Thrasymachus's response is a snort of derision – how could anyone be so naive? But the example he uses strikes a chilling contemporary note at the time of writing (in the middle of the foot and mouth epidemic in England in 2001). Shepherds and herdsmen, he says, only fatten their flocks for the good of their masters and themselves – they are not concerned with the animals' welfare.

Thrasymachus moves to a different tack, changing back from the big picture of political justice to the fate of the just man. Has Socrates not noticed that the just man always comes off worse than the unjust? He'll be duped in business, he'll pay more tax; he'll even earn the enmity of his friends because he disdains nepotism. Plato's readers, both here and at the even more emphatic statement by Glaucon about the fate of the just man a little later, cannot fail to be aware of a huge dramatic irony: Socrates, according to Phaedo and therefore Plato 'the most just and upright man of those whom we have known,' was not only worsted but put to death by his fellow-citizens. Thrasymachus is at his most eloquent here, when he describes the extreme of injustice represented by tyranny:

> ## QUOTATION
> *When a man not only seizes the property of his fellow-citizens but captures and enslaves their persons also... he is called happy and highly favoured.* (344)

SOCRATES'S FIRST DEFENCE OF JUSTICE

There's something bracing about Thrasymachus's cynicism. It is certainly better than a mouthing of pieties. However, Socrates must try to prove that ruling is not tantamount to profiteering, and that justice is stronger and more profitable (in the true sense) than injustice. First of all he returns to the question of specific skills or arts (*technai*). His point here is that wage-earning or money-making are in some sense separate activities from skills or arts such as medicine. Some have thought this to be a quaint argument, but it could also be seen as rather profound and important. A frequent student response to the question 'Why did Shakespeare write plays?' is 'In order to make money'. No doubt Shakespeare was not indifferent to money (he became a rich man) but that answer is unsatisfactory in failing to differentiate between play-writing, highway robbery and pig-breeding. If a doctor is thinking about making money while treating a patient she is not exercising her skill in the proper manner. Whatever their skill or art people need to be paid; their specific skill or art does not consist in making money.

It is one of the most original moves in *The Republic* to apply this principle to government. True government is such a difficult and selfless skill that no good person will want to undertake it without payment. We will hear much more of this great theme of reluctant politicians:

> QUOTATION
>
> *Virtuous men... enter upon administration... not with any idea of coming upon a good thing, but as an unavoidable necessity... because they cannot find any person better or no worse than themselves, to whom they can commit it.* (347)

The next stages of the discussion show Thrasymachus twisting and turning, well and truly spitted on the relentless Socratic *elenchus*. It seems relatively easy for Socrates to show that justice is a good quality and injustice a bad one (Thrasymachus has tried to argue the reverse), then that justice, contrary to appearances and to Thrasymachus' worldly wisdom, is stronger than injustice (because unjust men will be constantly squabbling and betraying one another and thus unable to take part in any joint enterprise) and finally that the just man will be happier than the unjust because '*justice [is] the virtue of the soul*' (353). The wild beast has been tamed; Thrasymachus, whose blush at 350 seems to reveal that he has been arguing for effect as much as from conviction, offers little resistance.

Just as important, however, is the fact that Socrates's arguments, at best suggestive, at worst specious, are not truly convincing. Although he has tamed Thrasymachus, he has not truly persuaded him. More to the point, he has not persuaded his two principal interlocutors Glaucon and Adeimantus – and Socrates's persuasion or conversion of these two young men is the central project of *The Republic*. According to the Socratic principle of therapeutic philosophy, as to the modern practice of psychotherapy, there is no point in a teacher simply uttering truths. Truth must be proved in the heart and mind of the listener. In an arresting turn-around, young Glaucon, not satisfied by Socrates's 'snakecharmer's' silencing of Thrasymachus, takes it upon himself to cross-question the famous questioner.

GLAUCON AND ADEIMANTUS RESTATE THE CASE AGAINST JUSTICE

Glaucon claims to be a devil's advocate, restating the thesis that justice is not a good in itself, but a social convenience or necessity, and that those who practise it generally come off worse than those who practise its opposite. This thesis rests on the pessimistic view that men naturally desire to do wrong. A proof of that view is the famous story of Gyges's ring. Gyges was the Lydian shepherd who came upon a gold ring which could make him invisible at will. Gyges used its power to seduce the king's wife, murder the king and seize power. No one would be able to resist similar abuse of similar power – or if they did, they would be laughed to scorn. If such an unlikely character as the just man (who does not use his power to harm his fellows) ever emerges, the following fate awaits him:

> ## KEY QUOTATION
> *[He] will be scourged, racked, fettered, will have his eyes burnt out, and at last, after suffering every kind of torture, will be crucified, and thus learn that it is best to resolve, not to be, but to seem, just.* (362)

Glaucon's brother Adeimantus, the more reserved of the two main interlocutors, steps in here to emphasize and elaborate on the last point, that what really matters is having a reputation for justice, not being just. He shrewdly observes that fathers generally urge their sons to behave well not so much because of a real belief in the goodness of justice, but for reasons of social prestige. Furthermore, the service paid to justice is often no more than lip-service. In practice, the situation is as follows:

> ## QUOTATION
> *[People] do not hesitate to call wicked men happy, and to honour them both in public and in private, when they are rich or possess other sources of power, and on the other hand to treat with dishonour and contempt those who are in any way feeble or poor, even while they admit that the latter are better men than the former.* (364)

To make matters worse, this dire state of affairs appears to be sanctioned both by the poets and by the stories about the gods which either show the unjust prospering or illustrate easy ways of expiating wrong-doing. At this point Socrates has to concede that the defence of justice will be no easy task.

What has been established by the opening exchanges of *The Republic* – the most dramatic and the most genuinely dialogic section of the entire work? The first point is that justice has been proved to be worth arguing about – and arguing about in a serious, dialectic way rather than through displays of flashy rhetoric. Conventional ideas of justice as disguised self-interest or unthinking compliance with laws have been exposed in all their shallowness. Justice has also had to withstand nihilistic attacks which would reduce it to an impractical foolishness, not really worth talking about. Justice, as Socrates himself admits, has not been satisfactorily defined, though suggestive ideas about its nature have been proposed. These ideas cover a wide spectrum, from the social world to the make-up of the individual soul. The width of this spectrum, the recognition that justice must be tracked down both in the political sphere and in the heart of man, will determine the shape of the dialogue as it unfolds in the succeeding books. As it turns out justice may be the dialogue's holy grail or guiding star. The interlocutors will be drawn irresistibly towards it, though it may turn out to be ultimately unattainable.

3 Politics: building the just city

In the Cave myth, Plato presents about as dark a vision of a polity as any writer has imagined. Not only is the locale an underground cavern – completely lacking in the architectural glories with which Plato was surrounded in Athens – but the inhabitants or citizens are in chains. If the Cave represents the city, it is a place from which enlightened people will want to escape as quickly as possible, and to which they will return only reluctantly or upon compulsion. For a political writer – and in *The Republic* Plato is at least in part a political writer – Plato seems to have an extremely negative view of the *polis*. He did not have a high opinion, as we shall see, of Athenian

democracy; this, after all, was the political system which murdered his great teacher and friend. A famous quotation from the *Gorgias* sums up this disdain for what many have seen as a model city: '*Not moderation and uprightness, but harbours and dockyards and walls and tribute-money were what they filled the city with.*' (*Gorgias* 519). But then neither did Plato have a high opinion of any existing polity, with the possible exception of the military 'timarchy' (see Chapter 10) of Sparta.

WHY BUILD THE CITY?

Given all this, why, in the succeeding books of *The Republic*, does Socrates with Glaucon and Adeimantus decide to 'build the city'? Rather quaintly, Socrates suggests that as '*a city is larger than one man … justice may exist in larger proportions in the greater subject.*' So the purpose of city-building – or city-painting, as the process comes to be described – is not political in essence, but part of the larger over-arching project of discerning the elusive quarry, justice, whose full nature is not yet defined but which seems to reside both '*in individual mind[s]... and in an entire city.*' Socrates's suggestion also leaves open the possibility that the city is being constructed not so much as a bricks-and-mortar reality, but as a paradigm of a human soul.

It was Plato's pupil Aristotle who said that '*man is a political animal*'. The two philosophers would probably have pronounced this famous phrase with very different inflections. For Aristotle in *The Politics* (the book where he takes issue with Plato's *The Republic*), the *polis* is both a natural and a desirable outcome of the human power of speech:

> *The power of speech is intended to set forth... the just and the unjust. And it is a characteristic of man that he alone has any sense of good and evil, of just and unjust, and the association of living beings who have this sense makes a family and a state... He who founded the State was the greatest of benefactors.* (1253)

Plato and Socrates concede the necessity of some sort of community – man on his own in a state of nature simply cannot survive – but do not share Aristotle's cheerful optimism. Existing polities are greater or lesser evils. The jaundiced colouring of Plato's view of actual politics should always be borne in mind when reading *The Republic*. Perhaps it also accounts for the extreme sketchiness of the 'painting' of the city. If this is a work of political science, it omits key elements of politics: there is nothing on deliberation, policy-making, legislation or voting procedures. Indeed in one superbly offhand passage (425) Socrates asks, as regards '*all the regulations of the market, the police, the custom-house and the like: shall we condescend to legislate at all on such matters?*' Adeimantus hardly needs to reply '*no*'. Sketchy the picture may be: but it is also inspired, full of illuminating brushstrokes.

THE MINIMAL COMMUNITY

The first city sketched by Socrates is a rustic, vegetarian utopia governed by the principles of necessity, simplicity and specialization in trades. Humans need food, shelter and clothing. It is quickly agreed that it will better to have specialist farmers, masons, weavers and shoemakers than to have everyone being a jack-of-all-trades. The innocuous-seeming **principle of specialization** will have momentous consequences: the establishment of a class of politicians. Imports are also agreed to be necessary (few Greek city-states could hope to be self-sufficient). The community is expanded to include merchants, retailers, labourers (non-specialized), a market and a currency. This minimal community – not really a city, and not dissimilar from the dream of many contemporary 'greens' – draws forth from Socrates a lyrical passage in praise of the simple life, and especially vegetarian feasting, the tone of which may be gently ironic. But where justice might be found here is not clear, except as Adeimantus suggests that it might be '*discoverable somewhere in the mutual relations*' of the inhabitants.

THE CIVILIZED CITY

In any case, Glaucon is not prepared to put up with this degree of rustic simplicity (especially the diet of peas and beans). He accuses Socrates of founding '*a community of swine.*' Plan one – the vegetarian utopia which according to Socrates represents the healthy community – must give way to plan two: the 'civilized city' with all the luxuries, red meat,

> **KEY ARGUMENT**
>
> Indulgence in such luxuries will lead to *the unbounded acquisition of wealth*, which in turn will mean coveting neighbours' land and thus, inevitably, war.

theatre, dancing, flute-girls, to which a sensual young man like Glaucon is naturally attracted but which Socrates considers fevered and unhealthy.

FROM LUXURY AND WAR TO SOLDIERS TO GUARDIANS

So, luxury and war, as opposed to simplicity and peace, are the governing forces of the civilized city – as perhaps they seemed the key characteristics of the magnificent but troubled city-state of Athens to the youthful Plato. War, according to the principle of specialization in trades which is reiterated, means a class of trained soldiers. At this point perhaps the most fateful move in the entire *Republic* is made – but so silently that its importance escapes most commentators. The soldiers turn into guardians (*phylakes*).

Plato does not explain why there should be a military hegemony in his 'ideal state'. The idea seems to come from Sparta, which was a military aristocracy in which '*the details of daily life were all strictly regulated with a view to the maintenance of perfect military efficiency*' (H. D. P. Lee, Penguin Classics translation, p.19). The guardians just appear; they are presented as a *fait accompli*, and one which has infuriated and scandalized many readers of *The Republic.* Not only that, but Socrates and Plato never ask the Roman satirist Juvenal's famous question, 'Who shall guard the guards themselves?'

> **KEYWORD**
>
> Guards to guardians: The move turns on two meanings of the Greek word *phylax* – guard and guardian. Socrates is talking about the need for soldiers to be highly skilled; the next moment he envisages '*the importance of the work which these guardians have to do*' as concerning not just the defence but the 'guardianship of the state.' The guardians – who become a class and the only sector of the community Plato is really interested in – emerge from a military context.

THE NATURE OF GUARDIANSHIP: PHILOSOPHICAL DOGS

However questionable the way they are imposed on the State, the guardians turn out to be rather different from the jack-booted fascists some critics have made them into. In fact, Socrates suggests that they should partake of the attributes of two apparently incompatible kinds of creature – dogs and philosophers. The good qualities of dogs are quickness of perception, speed, strength and bravery. But here a danger is obvious: dogs can be savage. The guardians '*certainly ought to be gentle to their friends, and dangerous only to their enemies.*' However, dogs do in fact have the faculty of distinguishing friends and enemies, which is a sort of philosophical faculty – it presupposes a kind of knowledge or wisdom. So '*the man whose natural gifts promise to make him a perfect guardian of the state will be philosophical, high-spirited, swift-footed and strong.*' This step completes the earlier one in which guards became guardians. Here the agenda of *The Republic* is well and truly set: it will concern the education of the guardians, how to make rulers truly philosophical.

The first stage in the educational programme concerning moral and physical education is dealt with in the next sections of *The Republic*, which we will consider in Chapter 4. Here we will stay with Socrates' discussion of the nature of guardianship, the division of the guardian class into two distinct sections and the relations of the guardians to other classes in the ideal state.

A division in the guardian class has seemed inevitable, despite the zany attraction of philosophical dogs. What would be the advantage of philosophers with a remarkable turn of speed, or dogs with sophisticated reasoning skills? In fact, the division is introduced by enunciating a principle which is reiterated time and time again:

KEY QUOTATION

We must select from the whole body of guardians those individuals who appear to us, after due observation, to be remarkable above others in the zeal with which, through their whole lives, they have done what they thought advantageous to the [community]. (412 – my emphasis)

Now we have a two-tier class of guardians: the most community-minded will be educated to take on the responsibility of ruling, while the others, called auxiliaries (a somewhat sinister-sounding term) will, in ways which Plato never clearly explains 'support the resolutions of the rulers.'

THE NOBLE LIE

It is at this point – where you might well think that Socrates is getting into very deep or mirky water – that we come to one of *The Republic*'s most notorious inventions, the so-called 'noble lie' or Foundation Myth. The 'lie' has also been translated as the 'magnificent myth' but the Greek word used is *pseudos*, which Plato almost invariably uses to mean 'falsehood', and it is reinforced by the passive participle *pseudomenous* meaning 'deceived', referring to its recipients. So what is this 'falsehood' which Socrates admits he is embarrassed to reveal to Glaucon and Adeimantus? Simply put, the lie is an official story or piece of state propaganda which relates that, instead of being educated by human agency, the inhabitants of the ideal state were fully formed, together with their accoutrements, in the depths of the earth. Furthermore, mother earth made up their composition in terms of metals, which in turn determined their position in the class structure: **gold** for guardian-rulers, **silver** for guardian-auxiliaries and **bronze** for all the rest (artisans, farmers, merchants, labourers).

CRITICISMS AND JUSTIFICATIONS OF THE NOBLE LIE

The lie has two main (highly questionable) purposes: to attach citizens by visceral ties to their native land or state, and to make palatable a class structure which rigidly separates rulers and ruled. It is not a *caste* structure: the lie makes clear that it is possible, though unlikely, for 'gold' children to be born to silver or bronze parents, or any of the other possible permutations, and that the appropriate educational and social consequences should follow. For many commentators this is not so much a noble lie as an ignoble piece of propaganda. In its favour you could argue first that it is presented with scrupulous candour, and second that its 'falseness', or the Phoenician quality Socrates alludes to, is the sweetening of the bitter pill of truth, namely that people are not born equal in ability. Other questions arise: why should anyone have a monopoly on telling such lies? If the lie is arbitrary (not based on reason), why should it not be replaced or accompanied by other lies? And why do Socrates and Plato so strongly endorse nationalism (attachment to native land) when later they will propose revolutionary measures to weaken attachment to family?

LIVING CONDITIONS OF THE GUARDIANS

Another of the subtle, or surreptitious moves in *The Republic* occurs at 415. The noble lie has been broadcast and the citizens are to be conducted to their living-quarters:

> QUOTATION
> *When we have armed these children of the soil, let us lead them forward under the command of their officers, till they arrive at the city: then let them look around to discover the most eligible position for their camp.*

The 'them' in the first part of this sentence seems to refer to the whole citizen body; the 'them' in the second part to the guardians alone. Is this a Freudian slip, revealing Plato's overwhelming preoccupation with the ruling class? Is it calculated, another sort of noble or ignoble device (*mechane*) being practised on the reader?

As regards the guardians' living conditions, Socrates proposes an austere military-style regimen which one might call in every sense Spartan.

> QUOTATION
> *No one should possess any private property, if it can possibly be avoided... they should attend common messes and live together as men do in a camp... to them, as distinguished from the rest of the people, it is forbidden to handle or touch gold or silver.*

The guardians will be paid a minimal wage to cover necessities.

HAPPINESS, WEALTH AND POVERTY

Adeimantus breaks in here with a heartfelt cry: '*What defence will you make, Socrates, if any one protests that you are not making the men of this class particularly happy?*' He was to be seconded by Aristotle, one of *The Republic*'s most astute critics: '*If the guardians are not happy, who are? Surely not the artisans, or the common people.*' (*Politics* 1264b). Socrates' answer is relentless:

> QUOTATION
> *Our object in the construction of the state is not to make any one class preeminently happy, but to make the whole state as happy as it can be made.*

And furthermore, a regime of unrestrained hedonism would not in the end lead to happiness: potters stretched on couches before the fire would no longer be fulfilling their function as potters. This leads to a more general reflection on wealth and poverty. Both are undesirable: '*the former produces luxury and idleness... and the latter meanness and bad workmanship.*' Where wealth and poverty are extreme, '*there are two cities, hostile one to the other, the city of the poor and the city of the rich.*' Here Socrates might be talking about the favelas or shanty-towns which look down on the wealthy beach-side districts of Copacabana and Ipanema in Rio de Janeiro, or about the British inner-city neighbourhoods which burned in 1981.

At this point, however, all roads lead to education. The point of imposing such an austere lifestyle on the guardians and auxiliaries was to discourage them from behaving more like 'wolves than dogs' and preying on their fellow citizens. Even more important than military-style camps and messes for the guardians and auxiliaries is the '*right sort of education...[which] will be most effectual in rendering them gentle to one another, and to those whom they guard*' (416).

4 Education and censorship

As with so much else in *The Republic*, Socrates's most profound thoughts on education are crystallized around the Cave image. Just after the passage describing the way eyes may be confused in two ways – '*by sudden transitions either from light to darkness or from darkness to light*' – Socrates, as if experiencing some inner illumination himself, has a piercing insight into what is perhaps the key theme of *The Republic*:

KEY QUOTATION

The real nature of education is at variance with the account given of it by... professors, who pretend... to infuse into the mind a knowledge of which it was destitute, just as sight might be instilled into blinded eyes... our present argument shows us that there is a faculty residing in the soul of each person, and an instrument enabling each of us to learn... [and] this faculty or this instrument [must] be wheeled round, in company with the entire soul, from the perishing world, until it be enabled to endure contemplation of the real world and the brightest part thereof. (518)

At this enlightened moment, education will be found to consist not in the 'chalking up' of knowledge or information or even skill onto a blank slate, but in the reorientation of sight, mind and soul. Justice in the community will surely depend on the extent to which the minds of rulers – and others – are oriented towards the brightest part of the real world which is goodness.

THE OVERRIDING IMPORTANCE OF EDUCATION

In Books 2 and 3, Socrates has not yet delved far enough into the nature of the soul, knowledge and reality to reach that clarity of insight. However, he already has an inkling of the overriding importance of education. At 376, after sketching the 'philosophical dog' character of the guardians, Socrates asks, *'In what manner shall we rear and educate them?'* Later, at 423, in a statement that is re-echoed throughout *The Republic*, he suggests to Adeimantus: *'The one great point... [is] education and rearing,'* and at 425, *'It is probable... that the bent given by education will determine all that follows.'* Education is so important that it must become a concern of the community as a whole. Plato, who ran a university for rich young men, was one of the first proponents of state education. Socrates may not yet know exactly how education relates to the main theme of justice, but:

> QUOTATION
> *In every work the beginning is the most important, especially in dealing with anything young and tender... for that is the time when any impression, which one may desire to communicate, is most readily stamped and taken.* (377)

Notice how different this imagery of imprinting is from the later 'wheeling round' or conversion.

EDUCATION AS THE CONTEXT OF *THE REPUBLIC*

Education is not only a key theme in *The Republic*, it is also the book's context. Plato was himself an educationalist and the philosophy he propounded and taught was based on the teachings of a man, Socrates, who paradoxically or ironically claimed not to be a teacher. The entire dialogue embodies a kind of teaching, which is also a therapy: the highest kind of teaching, as Socrates will maintain in Book 7, which he terms dialectic – a free dialogic questioning which will not rest until it has found, or better, arrived at a sharing of, the true principles of knowledge. In Book 1 this Socratic method of teaching via questioning has been contrasted with the Sophistic approach of Thrasymachus, which consists in dazzling an audience with startling theories.

DOES IT MATTER WHAT STORIES WE TELL OUR CHILDREN?

The focus in Books 2 and 3 is on literary, musical and physical education at what we would call secondary level. Above all, Socrates is concerned with the moral effect of the stories and the music to which young people are exposed. Perhaps we should say ethical rather than moral, remembering that ethical is derived from the Greek word *ethos*, meaning character. Socratic education in Books 2 and 3 is avowedly ethical: its aim is to produce and foster good character.

We should remember that the stories about the gods and heroes told by the Greek poets, above all Homer, were more than simply literature. Homer's *Iliad* and *Odyssey*, it has often been said, were the ancient Greek bible. We have already seen in the cases of Cephalus and Polemarchus how quotations from the poets might be used to give spurious authority to dubious moral precepts. By questioning the authority of the poets, Plato and Socrates are attacking a sort of conventional 'wisdom' which has ceased to be wise.

Gods and heroes behaving badly

Socrates seems particularly exercised about two kinds of stories: those which show the gods behaving badly (and getting away with it), and those which show heroes indulging in grief, fear of death or sensual excess. In the first case, the concern is not just that such stories will have a bad effect on children's characters, but that they demonstrate a deep confusion about ultimate realities. If God is by definition good and unchanging, how can gods be shown to be bad and changeable? Here, as often in *The Republic*, Socrates seems to anticipate Christian theology and to be at odds with traditional Greek polytheism. In the second case, the emphasis is on encouraging heroic, manly, martial qualities, and discouraging 'womanly' habits of indulging in emotion. Moving from content to form, Socrates argues that mimetic, representational poetry, including drama, is by definition suspect, since *'the same person [cannot] imitate many things as well as he can imitate one.'* (394)

Music and physical education

This ethical emphasis applies also to Socrates's strictures on music – the banning of dirges and laments, 'languid' modes or harmonies such as Ionian and Lydian, and certain instruments such as the harp and flute – and the recommendations for a *'careful training in gymnastics'.*

Music and Ethics

The ethical effect of music was taken very seriously by the Greeks: Aristotle's *Politics* ends with a long section on music, agreeing with Socrates on the banning of flutes (too exciting) but disagreeing about the retention of the Phrygian mode (too exciting once again). Music and harmony are to be valued not just for their own sake, but because they shadow forth the harmony of soul and body. *'The truly musical person will love those who combine most perfectly moral and physical beauty, but will not love anyone in whom there is dissonance.'* (402)

When it comes to physical education, Socrates recommends a *'simple moderate system.'* Music and gymnastics are seen as complementary. Excessive emphasis on physical training will produce a rough, philistine character, while too much music will produce sinewless softness and irritability.

ON CENSORSHIP: PLATO AND HIS CRITICS

The severe and puritanical censorship proposed in this section of *The Republic* will probably seem repugnant to modern liberal sensibilities. Some of the most powerful counter-arguments were voiced by Milton in *Areopagitica* (1644), and later by John Stuart Mill in *On Liberty* (1859). Milton, who recognized *The Republic* as an essentially 'Atlantick and Eutopian' polity, never designed to be realized, saw that Plato's censoring of literature and music necessarily '*pulls along with it so many other kinds of licencing, as will make us all ridiculous and weary.*' There will be an absurd proliferation of censors, and who will censor the censors themselves? And ultimately, the question of censorship raises the larger question of truth; for Milton and Mill, truth as it may be found in this world is plural and mixed; for Socrates (in *The Republic* at least) and Plato, it seems that unmixed knowledge of an indivisible truth can be attained by the truly enlightened man or woman.

Some have wondered if Socrates is not being a shade ironic. His recommendations would certainly appear to lead to the most boring imaginable kind of art: stories of unadulterated virtuousness. But though the censorship may be over the top, it surely raises questions pertinent to our time. Censorship is, after all, practised in contemporary societies including western liberal ones. Our criteria for censorship are negative ones: they do not decide on whether the content of stories is morally beneficial, but merely draw the line at certain graphic representations of sex and violence in the media of cinema, television and video. Why should these areas be singled out, as opposed to say representations of cheating, lying or other more subtle forms of misbehaviour? Is there not something rather hypocritical in the censoring of extreme or hardcore sex and violence when sex and violence in supposedly more acceptable forms appear to be the mainsprings of so many films, video games and other forms of entertainment? And are we doing our children a favour by imposing few restrictions on the kind of material they are exposed to? Are we in fact exercising our responsibilities as parents by leaving them in the hands of unscrupulous entertainment providers who see our children merely as a market ripe for exploitation?

ETHICAL EDUCATION

Finally, we might pause to observe some other differences between current theories of education and those sketched in Books 2 and 3 of *The Republic*. Much of current mainstream thinking on education is based on the idea of the acquisition of useful skills. Reading, writing, arithmetic and computer skills are taught not primarily to mould good character (or as good ends in themselves) but to equip children with ways of earning a living. Plato stands at the opposite extreme here: his guardians, of course, will not be called upon to earn their living – they will be supported by the rest of the community. His ethical education might seem impractical, but it could serve to make us question the ultimate ends of our devotion to 'usefulness'. If we are moulding our children to become smoothly functioning parts of an economic machine, are we not only denying them their autonomy, but also foreclosing on the possibility of judging the goodness of the 'economic progress' to which the educational system has become a servant?

5 Psychology: the divided soul

At the end of the Cave myth, Socrates discerns the essence of the educational and therapeutic task which is the unavoidable duty and calling of the philosopher:

> QUOTATION
>
> *This is a question involving not the mere turning of a shell, but the* revolution of a soul, *which is traversing a road leading from a kind of night-like day up to a true day of real existence.* (521 – my emphasis)

The key term, *psyche*, which encompasses both mind and soul and is radically distinct from the mortal body (*soma*) has been given remarkably little attention in the first few books of *The Republic*. When Socrates says at 353 '*Did we not grant that justice was a virtue of the soul?*' he is not being quite accurate: what had been agreed at 350 was that justice was equivalent to virtue and wisdom, but nothing was said there about soul. The importance of music in education had to do with the instilling or fostering of **harmony in the soul**: this is why:

> QUOTATION
>
> *We attach such supreme importance to a musical education, because rhythm and harmony sink most deeply into the recesses of the soul... making a man graceful if he rightly nurtured, but if not, the reverse.* (401)

THE NATURE OF PSYCHE

The time has clearly come to look more closely at the nature of *psyche*. *Psyche* is the locus of individual goodness, just as *polis* is the locus of communal justice. Before doing this, however, Socrates feels it is time to take stock and consider whether the conversation about politics and education has not lost touch with its main theme of justice. Has the city been properly founded? If so, it should rejoice in four key qualities (later known as the cardinal virtues): wisdom, courage, discipline and justice. Rather mysteriously, Socrates suggests that if the other three qualities are defined, justice will be identified as 'what is left over'.

The first two seem to be in place – they are accounted for by the good judgement of the guardians and the bravery of the auxiliaries. Discipline deserves closer attention – in fact, analysis of discipline will provide key insights into the nature of the soul. What does it mean to say that someone is 'master of himself'? Who is mastering whom? Socrates continues:

KEY QUOTATION

The meaning of the expression [appears to be] that in the man himself, that is in his soul, there resides a good principle and a bad, and when the naturally good principle is master of the bad, this state of things is described by the term 'master of himself'... (431).

THE SOUL DIVIDED AGAINST ITSELF

The idea that the soul is not a unity, that the soul and therefore a man can be 'divided against himself', is a momentous one, which links Plato with Freud and sets him against other thinkers from the Stoics onwards who have argued that there is something incoherent about the notion of a divided soul. On one level there is nothing abstruse about this. When developing his own theory about parts of the soul, Freud commented that the theoretical division into an 'I' (ego) and an 'it' (id) – Freud later added an 'above-I' or superego – reflected ordinary human ways of speaking about mental experience. People seem to experience one part of themselves being overcome by another part and say 'it was stronger than me.' But Socrates, recognising that an important principle is at stake here, approaches the question of the possible division of the soul with great caution and what might seem unnecessary logical quibbling. Instead of starting with an example drawn from experience, he must first prove in abstract terms that it is:

> QUOTATION
>
> *impossible that the same thing should, at the same time, with the same part of itself, in reference to the same object, be doing two opposite things.* (439)

All this becomes easier to understand when we take a particular case. For example, '*Can we [not] say that people are sometimes thirsty, and yet do not wish to drink?*' This shows that '*their soul contains one principle which commands, and another which forbids them to drink.*' Furthermore, that: '*Whenever the authority which forbids such indulgences grows up in the soul, [it is] engendered there by reasoning; while the powers which... draw the mind towards them, owe their presence to passive and morbid states?*' Here we have the basis for the primary division into two parts: the reasoning element (*to logistikon*) and the 'irrational and concupiscent' element, 'the ally of sundry indulgences and pleasures' (*to epithumetikon*).

THE THREE PARTS OF THE SOUL

Is there a third element in the mind or soul, something we might call indignation or righteous anger (*ho thumos*)? Socrates recalls the story of a certain Leontion, who was walking up from the Piraeus when he noticed '*some dead bodies on the ground, and the executioner standing by them.'* He experienced a conflict, not unfamiliar to those who pass the scenes of gory accidents: *'a desire to look at them, and [a] loathing [of the] thought.'* This leads him to cover 'his eyes

---

QUOTATION

... till at length, overmastered by the desire, he opened his eyes wide with his fingers, and running up to the bodies, exclaimed, 'There! you wretches! gaze your fill at the beautiful spectacle!' (440)

The anger that Leontion feels is clearly to be distinguished from the desire which it is directed against. It seems to be a sort of spiritedness, the quality which makes someone 'boil and chafe' when she thinks she *'is wronged... and whatever extremities of hunger and cold [she] may have to suffer... endure till [she] conquers, never ceasing from [her] noble efforts, till [she] has either gained [her] point or perished in the attempt.'* But is this spiritedness, which seems always to fight on the side of reason, actually to be distinguished from the reasoning element? Socrates thinks that it is:

QUOTATION

Little children from their very birth have... plenty of spirit, whereas reason is a principle to which most men only attain after many years, and some, in my opinion, never. (441)

The three-fold division of the soul rather conveniently (too conveniently?) echoes the tripartite class structure of the city. Socrates can now go back to an earlier, tentative definition of the just city, as one in which *'the three classes of characters [are] severally occupied in doing their proper work.'* (435). This apparently unambitious idea of 'minding one's own business' can then be applied to the balance of elements in the individual soul:

> ## KEY QUOTATION
>
> *... so that the just man will not permit the several principles within him to do any work but their own, nor allow the distinct classes in his soul to interfere with each other, but will really set his house in order; and having gained the mastery over himself, will so regulate his own character as to be on good terms with himself, and to set those three principles in tune together, as if they were... three chords of a harmony. (443)*

At this point Socrates, Glaucon and Adeimantus seem to feel they have pretty much succeeded in the task set near the beginning of the dialogue. Not only has a working definition of justice has been arrived at, but a correspondence has been found to hold between justice in the city and justice or goodness in the soul. All that seems left to do is to prove once and for all that justice pays better than injustice, and then to survey the various kinds of bad government which prevail both in cities and individuals. That survey will be carried out in Books 8 and 9, but only after a vast double digression which contains some of *The Republic*'s, and Western thought's, most daring and most profound philosophical flights.

PLATO AND FREUD

One explanation for the 'false ending' of *The Republic* could be that the psychological discussion has opened up a more prolific can of worms than Socrates is prepared, at this stage, to admit. Here we can draw parallels with Freud. For both thinkers the dark and irrational element of the soul seems 'larger' and more powerful than the other two: '*the concupiscent principle... in every man forms the largest portion of the soul, and is by nature most insatiably covetous.*' (442) For Freud, in his essay of 1926, 'The Question of Lay Analysis' (for which, incidentally, he chose the form of a Platonic dialogue) the 'it,' the self's seething, unconscious core, source of all the energies which drive the human being, is a *'mental region more extensive, more imposing and more obscure than the "I".* (Freud, Sigmund *The Essentials of Psychoanalysis*, Harmondsworth: Penguin, 1986, p.17)

Both Plato and Freud are rationalists who believe that the irrational part of the soul, which is the largest and strongest part, must somehow be tamed or befriended by the reasoning part. But this idea poses considerable conceptual difficulties. Pascal said that *'the heart has its reasons, of which reason has no knowledge at all.'* One difficulty concerns the negotiations which might take place between the different parts of the soul. Might not reason and appetite, or the 'I' and the 'it', speak mutually incomprehensible languages? This difficulty is compounded if, in Freudian terms, the 'it' is an unconscious area, to which we only have access through weird events like dreams and slips of the tongue.

At the end of Book 9 of *The Republic*, Socrates comes up with a striking image for the 'irrational and concupiscent element' of the soul: *'a motley, many-headed monster, furnished with a ring of heads of tame and wild animals,'* which the monster can turn into at will. Alongside the monster are a lion and a man, representing 'spiritedness' and reason. The man appears to have quite a task on his hands; an alliance with the lion is an obvious first step in taming the fearsome many-headed monster (compared also to the terrifying mythical creatures Scylla and Cerberus), but this therapy seems like a labour of Hercules, not a job for an ordinary human being.

6 Women, family and war

Together with the Cave myth, Book 5 of *The Republic*, in which Socrates discusses the intellectual and moral equality of women with men and arrangements for the communal begetting and rearing of children, is probably the most famous part of the entire great work. The theme is of perennial and direct human interest – no accident that Socrates' young male interlocutors force these issues into the dialogue at this dramatic juncture – and the treatment is radical, at times inspiring and at times shocking. Generations of readers from Aristotle to Aldous Huxley and beyond have been provoked and scandalized by the ideas proposed here: this is one part of *The Republic* which no one can, or indeed wants to, ignore.

Many readers, however, have succeeded in ignoring the very careful qualifications and hesitations with which Socrates flags and fences this section. There is a paradox; the section includes some of the most detailed and apparently practical proposals put forward anywhere in *The Republic*, and yet at the same time we are warned in no uncertain terms that these proposals represent a kind of day-dreaming, and above all others should not be subjected to immediate questioning concerning their feasibility. With regard to the community of women and children, Socrates warns Glaucon:

> ## QUOTATION
> *It is no easy matter... to discuss this question for it is beset by incredulity... In the first place, the practicability of our plans will not be believed; and in the next place, supposing them to be most completely carried out, their desirableness will be questioned.* (451)

Socrates goes further; in this matter he is broaching '*a theory... while... in the position of a doubting inquirer*': it would be a terrible thing to '*miss one's footing upon the truth*' and '*drag down*' one's fellow inquirers into error.

THE EQUALITY OF WOMEN

Glaucon acquits Socrates on the charge of misleading him and others (an obvious reference to the trial in 399 BC in which the outcome was tragically different) and Socrates proceeds to the first question, or 'wave':

KEY QUOTATION

Whether the nature of the human female is such as to enable her to share in all the employments of the male, or whether she is wholly unequal to any, or equal to some and not to others. **"**
(453)

It is quite clear in the succeeding discussion, one of the most noble and progressive examples of reasoning in *The Republic*, that the prevailing assumption in this context is that women are not only physically weaker than men but also intellectually and morally inferior. Socrates exposes this as an unjustified assumption, based on a lazy failure to examine different senses of the word nature (*physis*).

Women and men are fundamentally different only in their physical, or more precisely their reproductive nature; there is no fundamental difference regarding their ability to perform the various arts and occupations of the city. The conclusion is unequivocal and of epoch-making importance:

KEY QUOTATION

None of the occupations which comprehend the ordering of the state belong to woman as woman, nor yet to man as man; but natural gifts are to be found here and there, in both sexes alike; and, so far as her nature is concerned, the woman is admissible to all pursuits as well as the man. (455) **"**

As far as guardianship is concerned – remembering that all the above discussion is confined to arrangements within the guardian class – women are capable both of the 'love of wisdom' (*philosophia*) and the spiritedness or moral courage (*thumos*) which are the prime qualifications of the guardians proper and the auxiliaries.

COMMUNAL ARRANGEMENTS FOR CHILD-BEGETTING AND REARING; SELECTIVE BREEDING

Controversial as the idea of the fundamental equality of women with men might be, Socrates knows that his proposals for the complete abolition of the family (so that '*no-one shall have a wife of his own*') and its replacement with a communal system of child-raising (so that '*the parent shall not know his child, nor the child his parent*') are nothing short of scandalous. It is at this point that he asks to be allowed to indulge in what one might call 'idle speculation', '*to avoid the fatigue of thinking whether [these] wishes are practicable or not.*' (458)

What is most disturbing about this speculation may be not so much that it is impossibly far-fetched, but that it comes uncomfortably close to twentieth-century historical realities. Abolition of the family was proposed in the early days of Soviet communism and became a reality in the Israeli kibbutz movement. As for selective breeding or eugenics, this was championed by an extraordinary range of thinkers and politicians in the first half of the twentieth century, from idealistic socialists to Nazis. Modern developments of genetic engineering and cloning are currently subjects of intense debate. The proposals for the elimination of children born to parents who are too old, or are the offspring of incestuous unions, might seem especially callous, but might be compared with our practices of routine screening and abortion.

It was this section of *The Republic* which provoked Aldous Huxley to write *Brave New World* (1932), his dystopian satire about a society of totalitarian hedonism, controlled by eugenics, propaganda and drugs. There is in fact an almost novelistic quality about Book 5 of

The Republic, a fictional charm, which has led Julius Elias (see Further Reading) to wonder whether we should not consider this as a poetic myth rather than a cold-hearted, rational policy proposal.

Socrates's first concern is that the coming together of men and women in the ideal state should be as 'sacred' as possible. The fact that he immediately goes on to draw an analogy between selective breeding in animals and humans, though rebarbative to modern sensibilities, does not necessarily contradict this. The grand solemnity of the mating festivals he envisages is certainly far removed from a 'clinical' laboratory experiment, or the sterilization carried out in several twentieth-century states, including the USA, Sweden and Germany. More problematic is the frank admission that in order to bring together the 'best' of the men and women in order to produce 'excellent' offspring, the *'rulers will be compelled to have recourse to a good deal of falsehood and deceit for the benefit of their subjects.'* What this comes down to is the covert rigging of the lots which decide who shall sleep with whom: *'...these proceedings ought to be kept a secret from all but the magistrates themselves.'* For Elias, this is the only example of clear-cut deceit in *The Republic.*

COMMUNISM AND UNITY

Perhaps before deciding whether this famous passage shows Plato at his totalitarian worst, we should pause to consider his reasons for proposing the abolition of the conventional family. We are left in no doubt that the grand objective behind the proposals for community of women and children is the **fostering of unity, or a feeling of unity, in the city.**

KEY QUOTATION
Do we know... of any greater evil to the [city] than that which should tear it asunder, and make it into a multitude of [cities] rather than one? Or of any higher perfection than that which should bind it together, and make it one? (462)

Socrates's city will in effect be one big family, in which clannish self-interest will be replaced by a '*universal... feeling of sympathy*' spread throughout the community in which each citizen:

> QUOTATION
>
> *...must look upon every one whom they meet as either a brother, or a sister, or a father, or a mother, or a son, or a daughter, or one of the children or parents of these.* (463)

ARISTOTLE'S CRITICISMS – PLURALITY NOT UNITY

The first serious objections to these proposals were raised by Plato's most brilliant pupil, Aristotle, in Book II of the *Politics*. These are so detailed and so penetrating that they are worth considering at some length. Aristotle goes straight for the jugular, as it were, in questioning the desirability of unity in a state.

The state is a plurality... not made only of so many men, but of different kinds of men; for similars do not constitute a state. (1261 a)

As for the community of women and children, and common ownership of property, Aristotle is one of the first of those who, speaking from practical common sense rather than first principles, have argued that this system does not work:

That which is common to the greatest number has the least care bestowed upon it. Every one thinks chiefly of his own, hardly at all of the common interest; and only when he himself is concerned as an individual.

The 'common' children envisaged by Socrates:

... will be neglected by all alike... How much better it is to be the real cousin of somebody than to be a son after Plato's fashion! (1262 a)

In fact, '*the intention of Socrates in making these regulations about women and children*' (that of binding together the community with strong universal ties of friendship) '*would defeat itself:... in a state having women and children in common, love will be watery.*'

The debate between Plato and Aristotle on this point is one of the most far-reaching in Western intellectual history. At the beginning of the third millennium, after a century of mainly disastrous utopian political experimentation including the extravagantly cruel and costly experiences of Soviet and other forms of communism as well as Hitler and Mussolini's fascism, Aristotle's robust defence of private property and family ties might seem to have won the historical battle against the communistic proposals of Plato and Socrates.

Writing in the immediate aftermath of the political disaster of the mid-century, it was perhaps understandable that Karl Popper should brand Plato as a '*totalitarian party-politician, unsuccessful in his immediate and practical undertakings. but in the long run only too successful*' (*The Open Society and its Enemies*, London, Routledge, 1966, p.169), the intellectual godfather of Hitler and Stalin. But half a century later it is possible to see very considerable dangers in the dogmatic preference of the private over the public. Privatization of utilities and services in the UK and USA has had the predictable effect of prioritizing profits and shareholders' interests over the safety and benefit of the community as a whole which depends on those utilities and services.

Plato and Socrates were not necessarily wrong in predicting that a society or non-society (as in Mrs Thatcher's 'there is no such thing as society') based almost entirely on the self-interest of individuals and families might degenerate into two or more hostile 'cities', of the rich and the poor, the black and the white etc. Plato's political thinking did not extend beyond the *polis*, or Greek city-state; we are now faced with the challenges of globally interdependent economy and eco-system. In that context, however, Socrates's attempt to foster universal sympathy, echoed later by John Donne when he preached that 'no man is an island,' might seem more far-sighted than Aristotle's bland assumption that 'the common interest' will be routinely ignored.

HOW TO HUMANIZE WAR

The next part of Book 5 of *The Republic* deals with matters of war and foreign policy.

As we saw near the beginning of the work, Socrates assumes that war is an inevitable feature of the 'civilized city' which to him is already a corrupt degeneration of the healthy, minimal community. Given that assumption, with the exception of the recommendation, bizarre-seeming to most modern sensibilities, that children should be encouraged to be spectators of war, the aim of the discussion is to humanize and temper the barbarities of war. Greeks, Socrates argues, should neither enslave one another (the only reference to slavery in *The Republic*) nor devastate and burn land and houses. This last point is repeated several times in the space of a few pages:

> QUOTATION
> *Greeks... will not devastate Greece nor burn houses, nor admit that all the men, women and children in a city are their foes; always confining this name to those few who were the authors of the quarrel.* (471)

This repeated emphasis is no doubt partly the product of the experience of the Peloponnesian War, in which both Sparta and Athens were guilty of acts of atrocity against fellow Greeks. We could also compare this very early attempt to limit the destructiveness of war with the terrible extension of murderous destruction in the twentieth century, including genocide and the bombing of cities from the air. At this point in *The Republic*, Socrates still makes a distinction between Greeks, among whom these rules of war will apply, and barbarians (all those who do not speak Greek), to whom they do not. It is only after the long philosophical disquisition that Socrates can cast doubt on this distinction by suggesting that the truly just city could exist equally well among barbarians as among Greeks.

7 The rule of philosophy

Almost exactly at the midway point of the dialogue, just after the discussion of the equality of women, the family and war, *The Republic* experiences its gravest crisis. Socrates's young interlocutors are impatient: '*Let us try now,*' urges Glaucon, '*to convince ourselves of this, **that** the thing is practicable, and how it is practicable, leaving all other questions to themselves.*' (471 – translators' emphasis.) Socrates can only disappoint his friends: the relationship of the thought-adventure in which they have been engaged to feasibility in practice is more subtle and complex, and perhaps tragically flawed, than has so far been admitted.

The statement Socrates makes at 472 is one of the most important in the entire work:

> ## KEY QUOTATION
> *The design of our investigations into the nature of justice in itself, and the character of the perfectly just man, as well as the possibility of his existence, and likewise into the nature of injustice and the character of the perfectly unjust man, was to use them as patterns, so that by looking upon the two men, and observing how they might stand in relation to happiness and its opposite, we might be compelled to admit in our own case, that he who resembles them most closely in character, will also have a lot most closely resembling theirs: but it was not our intention to demonstrate the possibility of these things in practice.*

Here we seem worlds away from bricks-and-mortar city-building. The emphasis is clearly ethical more than political and there is a crucial change of focus: instead of looking outside, at the way things are organized in the city, Socrates is encouraging his interlocutors to

look inwards, to examine themselves and to see how they might come to resemble the kind of good person whose lineaments are being painted in *The Republic*.

Socrates is about to spring his greatest surprise, what he calls 'the third wave' and the one which is most likely to drown him in ridicule. Once again, his words, to which he asks his hearers to listen with special attention, deserve to be quoted at length:

> KEY QUOTATION
>
> *Unless it happens either that philosophers acquire the kingly power in states, or that those who are now called kings and potentates, be imbued with a sufficient measure of genuine philosophy, that is to say, unless political power and philosophy be united in the same person... there will be no deliverance, my dear Glaucon, for cities, nor yet, I believe, for the human race; neither can the commonwealth, which we have sketched in theory, ever till then grow into a possibility, and see the light of day.* (473)

One can imagine the consternation of Glaucon and the others at having this veritable tsunami sprung upon them. Everything, as far as the realization of the ideal state and the deliverance of mankind from evil and suffering are concerned, turns out to depend on something which has been only cursorily discussed as yet, but which will be subject of the next 50 or so pages, the core of *The Republic*. That something is philosophy. Obviously, it is time to define the beast.

WHAT IS PHILOSOPHY/WHO IS THE PHILOSOPHER?

One component of the Greek compound word *philosophia* has to do with love (*phileo*, I love, *philia*, love or friendship). The philosopher is a special sort of lover. Socrates starts the discussion in the realm of the (homo)-erotic, appealing to the sensuality of young Glaucon. Is not someone who loves boys '*in some way attracted and excited by the charms of all those who are in their bloom...?*' (474) Doesn't the same apply to the wine-lover, who finds '*some excuse or other to admire every kind of wine?*' Likewise:

> QUOTATION
> *The philosopher, or the lover of wisdom* [sophia], *is one who longs for wisdom, not particularly, but wholly... when a man is ready and willing to taste every kind of knowledge, and addresses himself joyfully to his studies with an appetite which can never be satiated, we shall justly call such a person a philosopher.* (475)

The philosopher is not a specialist in some particular field of knowledge, like a modern academic, but an insatiable, joyful polymath, a lover of all fields of knowledge.

THE PASSING SHOW VERSUS ESSENTIAL BEAUTY

At this point Glaucon asks a naive-seeming question: Are theatre-lovers philosophers? This may not be as foolish a question as it might sound, given the prominence of theatre in Athenian culture and the status of the great tragedians as profound thinkers and ethical teachers. At any rate, it gives Socrates the cue for a distinction of the utmost importance. The theatre presents a passing show of attractive, ever-changing spectacle. Theatre-lovers, like the denizens of the Cave (which is a kind of theatre), are entranced by the beauty of the spectacle but cannot see the essential nature of beauty – or the beauty of truth. Such a statement, of course, implies that there is such a thing as 'the essential nature of beauty.'

KNOWLEDGE VERSUS BELIEF

In what follows, Socrates often seems to be proceeding by dogmatic assertions rather than truly dialectic argument – a sign perhaps that the distinction between the true knowledge or understanding (*episteme*) of essential reality which is the goal of the philosopher and the inferior grasping of phenomena which he calls belief or opinion (*doxa*) is a sort of *a priori* in Plato's thinking. The distinction seems self-evident to Plato, yet he is aware that for most people it cannot be self-evident. Therefore, it must be argued for. All the same, we should note that these are provisional statements, part of an ongoing investigation.

At 475 Glaucon says:

> ## QUOTATION
> *[Philosophers are] those who love to see truth.*

Though true, this might be little more than a truism. Socrates tries again. The trouble with phenomena in the world is that their nature seems essentially mixed up. Though we can distinguish beauty and ugliness, justice and injustice, as absolutes in our minds, when we look around us we see phenomena which are both beautiful and ugly, people who are good and bad. People like theatre-lovers (and that means most people) who are predominantly sensual, who love 'sounds and colours and forms' will only see this 'mixed-up' reality which is both beautiful and ugly; they are not able to discern the **essences of things**. These people, according to Socrates, are not awake but dreaming: only the philosopher, who '*acknowledges an abstract beauty, and has the power to discern both this essence and the objects into which it enters*' (476) can be said to be awake.

The philosopher's power of discernment, Socrates asserts, constitutes knowledge. Knowledge can only pertain to that which exists.

> ## QUOTATION
> *What completely exists may be completely known, whereas that which has no existence at all must be wholly unknown.* (477)

That seems clear, but most of what goes on in the world, as we have seen, occupies a sort of middle ground between being and not-being. Likewise: '*The mass of notions, current among the mass of men, about beauty, justice, and the rest, roam about between the confines of pure existence and pure non-existence.*' (479) If knowledge is the faculty that pertains to what exists, there must be another faculty which pertains to this intermediate realm: that faculty is belief or opinion. Theatre-lovers cannot be called philosophers; they need another title – philodoxists, perhaps.

A late-night TV arts discussion programme might provide a contemporary context helpful for understanding Socrates's and Plato's knowledge/belief distinction. Two pundits express radically different opinions about the latest Bertolini film. For one it is a masterpiece, for the other the final proof that the aged director has lost his grip. Either one, though not both, of these opinions could be true, according to Socrates and Plato; what is lacking is the grounding and verifying of these opinions in some transcendent value or standard. It is not that all the opinions routinely exchanged in everyday life are false, but that without recourse to something beyond mere opinion there is no sure way of telling which are false and which are true. We will need to wait until the next section to find out what this ultimate arbiter might be.

THE CHARACTER OF THE PHILOSOPHER

Although Socrates and Plato's knowledge/belief distinction might seem rather abstract, it cannot in the end be separated from the characters of the lover of knowledge and the lover of spectacle. Nor should philosophy, ultimately, be separated from the governance of the city. Socrates must return to the character of the philosopher and flesh out the rather bare bones so far supplied. Philosophers are lovers of knowledge, but of a special sort: they are not amassers of information for the sake of information, but are:

> **QUOTATION**
> *... enamoured of all learning, that will reveal to them somewhat of the real and permanent existence, which is exempt from the vicissitudes of generation and decay.* (485)

The love of wisdom, as we call this special sort of knowledge, is always allied to a love of truth and a hatred of falsehood. Someone whose heart is set on wisdom and truth is unlikely to be concerned with the pleasures of the body; neither will he or she be '*anxious for money at any cost*,' petty-minded in any way or afraid of death. The qualities of the philosopher – or perhaps we should say the philosopher-ruler – are summed up as:

> **QUOTATION**
> *... manliness, loftiness of spirit, a quick apprehension and a good memory.* (490)

Adeimantus' objection

At this point Adeimantus steps in with one of the most interesting interventions in the entire *Republic*. He feels uneasy with the whole process of Socratic *elenchus*. Step by step it is hard to refute the great dialectician, but after a whole series of such steps you may suddenly find yourself in a seriously false position. The current situation is a case in point. Socrates has succeeded, apparently, in arguing that only philosophers have the requisite virtues and abilities to make them good rulers, when everyone knows in fact that philosophers are odd, vicious or useless.

THE FATE OF PHILOSOPHY

Critics through the centuries have detected a peculiarly personal tone in the next few pages of *The Republic*, in which Socrates discusses the sad state of philosophy in Athens, emanating more from the disillusioned Plato than the cheerfully ironic Socrates. If conditions are bad for philosophy and the philosopher in the city, especially the democratic city, there are two main reasons. Socrates comes up with one of his most striking analogies: he compares the city to a ship, with a captain who is bigger and stronger than the rest and a crew which spends its time squabbling. The captain stands for the people and the crew for politicians. In this unruly set-up the navigator, who might steer the ship on the right course, is not heeded. Indeed, there is no acknowledgement of the existence of the art and science of navigation. Likewise in the democratic city the true philosopher is not valued.

There is a further problem. The combination of qualities required for true philosophy is very rare: most people calling themselves philosophers are rogues, impostors or second-raters. Not only that, but the good qualities which mark out the philosophical nature carry in themselves the possibility of their own corruption.

At this point Socrates has one of his most far-sighted visions, of what we might call a politics of environment and quality:

> QUOTATION
>
> *In the case of all seeds, and of everything that grows, whether vegetable or animal, we know that whatever fails to find its appropriate nourishment, season and soil, will lack its proper virtues the more, in proportion as it is vigorous.* (491)

So, 'the finest natures get more harm, than those of an inferior sort, when exposed to an ungenial nutriment' – this last phrase being translated in Penguin as 'unfavourable environment'. This is the reason why 'minds, naturally of the finest order, if they happen to be ill-trained, become peculiarly wicked.' There are obvious and challenging implications here for both education – to be explored in the next sections – and therapy. In Alice Miller's influential account, the gifted child is especially at risk from an unnourishing kind of upbringing, because that child will so quickly perceive and deliver his or her parents' unhealthy expectations.

This is the idea of 'corruptio optimi pessima' (the worst kind of corruption is that of the best person) which resonates not only through history – one might think of the gifted minds who worked in the service of Nazism, or even the scientists such as Oppenheimer who joined the American nuclear bomb programme – but also in popular literary creations such as Tolkien's brilliant but corrupt white wizard Saruman or Conan Doyle's Moriarty. The figure whose shadow falls over these pages, commentators have agreed for centuries, is Socrates's friend Alcibiades, the charismatic and brilliant Athenian general who was partly responsible for the disastrous Sicilian expedition of 415–413 BC and later intrigued against Athens.

The tyranny of the popular

What exactly is the pernicious influence which corrupts the minds of such greatly gifted people? Are young persons corrupted by Sophists (another obvious reference to Socrates's trial) – or is not the real corrupting influence public praise and censure, which is a far more dangerous and powerful kind of Sophist? How can a young man 'retain his self-possession' when faced with the tumultuous clapping and booing of a popular assembly? Public opinion and pressure, and the threat of punishment, are more or less irresistible. The so-called Sophists, far from corrupters of the public, are in fact its servants – they 'teach nothing but the opinions of the majority.' This majority can be compared to a large, savage beast: the Sophistic teacher might study the creature's moods and become an expert animal-handler, but this handling would have nothing to do with true philosophical discernment of the essences of justice and injustice, beauty and ugliness etc. All this leads to a 'tyranny of the popular' not just in politics but also in art – which might seem eerily familiar to anyone who has followed British New Labour's courtship of 'the people' including the invocation of Princess Diana as 'the people's Princess' and the canonization of pop stars and artists of dubious worth.

Socrates and Plato's gloomy conclusion is that philosophy and democracy are more or less incompatible. The argument that the minds most suited to philosophy will be corrupted by public and peer-group pressure can be challenged – surely the susceptibility to this kind of pressure might represent an unphilosophical character flaw? It is hard not to see this as special pleading inspired by personal affection for the fallen Alcibiades. However, the picture of philosophy languishing in neglect, as the minds which should espouse it turn to more obviously lucrative pursuits, and of philosophers keeping a low profile for fear of being torn to pieces by the wild beast of populism, is a compelling and prophetic one.

Might there not be something radically wrong with Plato's dream of combining philosophical calling and political power in the same person? Immanuel Kant thought so:

That kings should become philosophers, or philosophers kings, is not likely to happen; nor would it be desirable, since the possession of power invariably debases the free judgement of reason. It is, however, indispensable that a king – or a kingly, i.e. self-ruling people – should not suppress *philosophers but leave them the right of public utterance. (quoted in Popper,* The Open Society and its Enemies, *London: Routledge, 1966, p.152)*

To be sure, there have been some questionable examples of people of a theoretical persuasion assuming political power: take Abimael Guzmán Reynoso, philosophy professor and leader of Peru's Sendero Luminoso. All the same, faced with democratic leaders whose sole interest often appears to be their own or their party's re-election, we can legitimately dream with Plato of a more far-sighted kind of leadership.

Socrates, at any rate, continues to dream. In a beautiful passage at the end of this section, he seems purged of the bitterness which was evident earlier. The rule of philosophy is not an impossibility, he repeats: what is necessary is a new approach both to the teaching of philosophy and to the removal of the prejudice against it among the many, who must not be bullied but won round gently. Most people are in fact amiable: the fault for the bad reputation of philosophy lies mainly with the pseudo-philosophers. The stakes are very high: only in this way will the god-like nature of humankind already noted by Homer (who described men as 'godly and godlike') be made to shine forth in a world governed by justice.

8 The good and the Cave

If the thought-adventure of *The Republic* resembles an arduous mountain-hike, we are now very close to the summit. At this high point – one of Western philosophy's loftiest peaks – Socrates speaks mainly in images. Rather than presenting arguments, he offers visions. The thinker who will banish poets from his ideal state speaks himself in poetry. One reason for this could be that he is not only talking about, but actually experiencing a kind of illumination.

THE IDEA OF GOOD

Philosophers, we have seen, are people who discern the true nature of things. But what makes this vision or discernment possible? Is there '*something higher than justice and those other things we have discussed?*' (504) His interlocutors, Socrates says, will have heard (from him, we presume, in earlier dialogues) about a higher something called '*the idea of good*' (often translated as '*the Form of the Good*'), which somehow '*blends with*' things and makes them '*useful and advantageous*'. But this good has never been defined satisfactorily. Some identify it with knowledge or pleasure; they are wrong. It is this '*good... which every soul pursues, as the end of all its actions, divining its existence, but perplexed and unable to apprehend satisfactorily its nature.*' Glaucon expects Socrates to be able to go further than these perplexed souls, but the philosopher holds back, seemingly perplexed himself: he must '*put aside all inquiry into the nature of the chief good*' (506), only being prepared to discuss '*that which appears to be an offshoot*' of it.

THE SUN AND THE GOOD

He is saying, in other words, that he can only offer a metaphor. He prefaces it by repeating one of his key distinctions, between the realm of appearances, seen by the eyes, and true realities or things as they really are, which can be apprehended only by the intellect. The metaphor uses the nature of seeing to convey something about reasoning. What is it that makes vision possible, aside from eyes and objects? The sun, obviously. The way in which the sun guarantees vision, allowing things to appear and be seen (and indeed to exist), is the equivalent, in the realm of the visible, to the way in which the idea of good guarantees reality and truth to ideas, forms or essences in the realm of the intellect, or pure reason. This is why the idea of good can be called the origin of knowledge and truth, and something which '*transcends... real existence in dignity and power.*' (509)

Plato's good may sound very abstruse and intellectual, but his 'idea of good' is closely related to goodness, which is far from a purely intellectual concept. Goodness is rather like the sun: omnipresent and essential to life, as the light and warmth which surround us, but also out of reach and impossible to look at directly. Only goodness can guide us in our search for knowledge and truth, to see things as they are. If we follow other guides, such as the desire for power, control over nature, or knowledge for its own sake, we will go astray. '*Goodness,*' as Iris Murdoch (*The Sovereignty of Good*, London: Routledge, 1970, p.93) has said, '*is connected with the attempt to see and respond to the world in the light of a virtuous consciousness.*' All this will become clearer when the sun metaphor is developed in the great allegory of the Cave.

KEY CONCEPT

The Divided Line: Socrates offers a diagram to help clarify the distinction between the visible and intelligible realms, the objects of sight and knowledge, and the faculties which apprehend those objects. This is the Divided Line. There is one main division into two sections – the visible and the intelligible. Each of those two sections is further subdivided into two. The visible is divided into the realm of shadows and images (apprehended by illusion, *eikasia*) and the realm of real, physical things such as animals, plants, objects (apprehended by belief or opinion, *pistis* – the word used here in preference to *doxa*). The division in the intelligible realms is more difficult to grasp: it is between the kind of mathematical or scientific reasoning (*dianoia*) which uses images or hypotheses to proceed to conclusions, without examining those images or hypotheses, and the superior kind of philosophical or dialectical reasoning (*noesis*) which proceeds from hypotheses or assumptions up to self-sufficient first principles. This last kind of reasoning will be discussed further in the next chapter.

THE CAVE

Now the metaphor of the sun and the diagram of the divided line are developed, illustrated and dramatized in *The Republic*'s most haunting myth or allegory. We are back where we started in this guide, in the flickering firelight of the Cave. Most people, we remember, spend their lives as chained prisoners, mesmerized by the play of shadows cast by images on a wall. Release from this condition (the realm of illusion) is difficult and gradual. The first stage of release consists in being able to turn round and see the fire, the light-source responsible for the shadows. (Iris Murdoch interprets the fire as the self, perpetually consumed in desire and sending out projections.) It may then be possible to see the real objects which cast the shadows. But the former prisoner who reaches this stage – that of belief or illusion – has a long and difficult ascent still to negotiate – the climb out of the cave into daylight or sunlight (the intelligible realm). The realities seen in this light will seem dazzlingly bright at first to someone used to the shadow-world. As for looking at the sun itself (the idea of good), that blinds normal human sight.

Release is seen as a **process of guidance, education or therapy**. It takes an enlightened person – someone who has somehow cast off her shackles, seen her own benighted situation and what causes it (ignorance or egoic desire), then accomplished the arduous ascent to daylight and true reality – to help reorient others. It is also the *calling* of that enlightened person, philosopher, educationalist, therapist or politician, to help reorient others. It might be very pleasant for a person who had escaped from the shadow-world of obsession with power, status, money and sex to spend their time in 'ivory-tower' philosophizing. However, the good or enlightened person experiences some kind of summons (perhaps a divine one, as in the case of Socrates) to go back down into the Cave to help her suffering fellow creatures. That summons has something to do with goodness. As the Jesuit priest and poet Gerard Manley Hopkins put it, '*the just man justices*' – that is, does active good in the world.

The re-descent is fraught with danger. The enlightened person will have difficulty readjusting to the shadowy light of the Cave. Having lost interest in shadows, she may appear stupid to the experts in shadows. When she tries to make people aware of the darkness of their situation, she will experience massive resistance and may even be killed, like Socrates. Resistance – the unwillingness of the individual to acknowledge uncomfortable truths – is one of the key concepts of Freudian psychoanalysis.

The metaphor of the sun and the allegory of the Cave are immensely rich in possible meanings and readings. Norman O. Brown, taking a lead from Melanie Klein, interprets the Cave as the mother's womb, into which the child, and the regressing adult, wish to return: *'We are still unborn; we are still in a cave; Plato's cave.'* (*Love's Body*, Berkeley: University of California Press, 1990). Jung warns against just such a Freudian reading, designed to prove *'that even the mind of Plato was deeply stuck in the levels of "infantile sexuality"'*, while missing the point of what the metaphor says about the *'the whole problem of the theory of cognition'* (*Contributions to Analytical Psychology*, London: Kegan Paul, Trench, Trubner, 1928, p.232).

Socrates and Plato wish to keep open the **political** reading as well as the educational and therapeutic. The enlightened and good people who return to the Cave will *'enter upon... administration as an unavoidable duty.'* The guardianship of these reluctant rulers has a chance of making the dream of the just city into a reality, unlike *'the phantom... life of our present states, which are mostly composed of men who fight among themselves for shadows.'* (520) Certainly, no process of educational or therapeutic enlightenment will be possible in certain dark and perverted regimes – as the experience of the twentieth century repeatedly showed. But the focus of the next sections will be on the very specialized higher education of the good and enlightened person who is also the philosopher.

9 Higher education

In the latter part of Book 7 of *The Republic*, Socrates sets out his proposals for the education of the philosopher. It is a rarefied and dauntingly abstract programme. Looking back on the earlier proposals for an ethical education in literature, music and gymnastics, Socrates is dismissive: such an education might foster '*a kind of harmoniousness... and measuredness*' of character, but had little to do with knowledge. Perhaps he is unfairly dismissive: he seems to be forgetting for a moment that character and knowledge are intimately connected. Only persons of especially good character are fitted for philosophy, whose ultimate goal is the good. Now Socrates seems bent uncompromisingly on reorienting only the very best minds towards the highest reality which is goodness. This does seem like an elitist programme. But we might compare it to a psychoanalytic or psychotherapeutic training. Only a few will measure up to the demands of such a training, but underlying the practice of the psychoanalyst or psychotherapist will be a belief in the possibility of reorienting or unshackling a faculty common to all human beings.

This is a two-stage programme. A series of mainly mathematical subjects, arithmetic, plane geometry, solid geometry, astronomy and harmonics, will be studied as the preparation for the ultimate philosophical discipline which is called dialectic. Why is there such a strong bias towards mathematical subjects? Mathematics, Socrates says at 523, is:

> KEY QUOTATION
>
> *by nature one of those studies leading to reflection... but no-one appears to make right use of it, as a thing which tends wholly to draw us towards real existence.*

UNITY AND DIFFICULTY

The pull towards 'real existence' exerted by abstract disciplines appears to work in two ways: first of all, the objects of these disciplines are eternal truths rather than passing, unreliable phenomena. Reasoning, for Plato and Socrates, is more reliable than perception. Optical and other sensory illusions occur, but no such illusion can cloud the purely reasoning mind. Secondly, there is something conducive to thought in the sheer difficulty of mathematics: puzzlement has a mentally stimulating effect. When there is an apparent contradiction, especially as regards unity and plurality:

QUOTATION

The mind will be compelled to puzzle over the difficulty, and stir up the inward faculty of thought to the investigation, and put the question, 'What after all is unity in itself?' (24–5)

DIALECTIC

The mathematical subjects are studied not so much as ends in themselves – and definitely not for anything as vulgar as the desire to succeed in business – but as preludes to the main theme or 'actual hymn' (531), the discipline of disciplines which is the philosophical inquiry called dialectic. If dialectic can be defined, Socrates and his interlocutors may finally be able to '*close* [their] *march, and rest from* [their] *journey.*' (532).

Dialectic as exemplified in *The Republic* is not a bald trotting-out of truths and arguments; it is essentially co-operative and depends on the assent – the free assent, not the brow-beaten subjugation – of other co-inquirers.

KEY CONCEPT

Dialectic: Dialectic is the process which is enacted in *The Republic* itself – the process of questioning which goes on and on until it reaches a point which is somehow beyond questioning – an 'ultimate beginning' or first principle which does not depend on other propositions but rests on its own self-sufficiency. Socrates and Plato call that first principle the idea of good.

Socrates and Plato claim that dialectical reason is superior to scientific reason because it rests not on hypotheses which are always open to question but on self-sufficient first principles. Sir Francis Bacon boldly challenged that claim, deciding, in order to 'ease man's estate' and achieve apparently quantifiable improvements in the human condition, to eschew first principles and embrace 'middle axioms' or testable hypotheses which would deliver useful knowledge. Now the amazing advances which Western science, freed of any obligation to 'the idea of good', has achieved over the last few centuries have come to seem increasingly dubious in terms of their ultimate value. Developments such as nuclear fission and fusion and animal and human cloning, or even something as apparently harmless as the mobile phone, appear dangerously double-edged, offering potentialities for both good and evil. Now no less than in ancient Athens, or perhaps especially now, some kind of ethically informed human reason – the Socratic and Platonic dialectic – is called for in order to adjudicate the ultimate good of scientific and technological 'usefulness'.

Bad government 10

Good government can only come about, according to Socrates, when philosophers rule in the city, or when those who rule have a thorough grounding in philosophy. The trail of justice or goodness (both in the individual soul and in the city) has led to an unlikely, or not so unlikely place – a philosophical school, not dissimilar to Plato's own Academy, where that grounding can be acquired. It will not be used for its own sake, but to help turn around the erroneous mind-sets of the suffering human beings who are chained in the Cave – thus achieving a revolution which is both ethical or psychological and political. There are all sorts of hazards: some philosophical minds carry the seeds of their own corruption; when the truly good people who are philosophers return from contemplation of eternal realities to the Cave/city, they may well be violently rejected, set upon and killed.

Good government, as Glaucon and Socrates ruefully acknowledge at 592, may be a pipedream, impossible to realize in practice. But to give up any idea of its realization leads to despair. Bad government, both within the individual psyche and in the city, is the prime source of the troubles and afflictions of mankind – and therefore worth sustained attention. In the conclusion of the main part of *The Republic*, Socrates makes good the promise made at the end of Book 4, to look at the four main types of bad government (the four '*distinctive forms of government*') which are also '*characters of mind*,' and finally to prove that justice pays better than injustice. Two questions are likely to occur to the reader here: first, why are there four types, not more or fewer (Aristotle in the *Politics* distinguishes several kinds of monarchy, oligarchy and democracy), and secondly, how exact can the correlation be between types of constitution and types of character?

Plato's Inferno

This section is structured as a descent or degeneration – a kind of inferno – starting with the least bad and leading down to the most terrible and destructive form of regime which, as most modern readers would probably agree with Socrates, is represented by tyranny. Much more surprising to modern readers is the placing of democracy in the penultimate position.

TIMARCHY

For Socrates and Plato the least bad form of government, which is also the first stage of degeneration from the ideal philosophocratic state, is the highly authoritarian type of state with a strong emphasis on military and competitive values thought of as the Spartan or Cretan type and given the name 'timarchy'.

Plato and Socrates claim that the good features of this kind of state are the respect for authority and physical training, while its drawbacks (not minor ones) include a rampant lust for money, though not yet as rampant as in oligarchy, an excessive emphasis on ambition and competition and the enslaving of one part of the population by another, together with excessively harsh treatment of the slaves by the 'masters.' In Ancient Sparta, the military, ruling caste declared war annually on the serfs or helots, so that the killing of a helot could be considered a justifiable act of war, not a crime.

The idea that such a system, which could be compared to the apartheid regime in South Africa, represents the least bad kind of government is hard to swallow. In defence of Plato, one can point out that timarchy is not presented as admirable, just less undesirable than the other types. The basic flaw of timarchy, as indeed of all the other kinds of bad government, for Plato, stems from lack of confidence in education; education is conducted '*not by persuasion but by force*', and does not contain a sufficient admixture of the musical element, '*the true muse that goes hand in hand with profound philosophical enquiry*'. (548) Equally, one might consider that timarchy's basic fault was cruelty.

OLIGARCHY

With oligarchy, next in the descending order of perverse regimes, we come to a much more familiar type of 'bad government'. The definition of oligarchy is:

> QUOTATION
>
> *... a constitution grounded upon property qualification... in which the wealthy rule, while the poor have no part in the government.* (550)

The motor which drives such a society is described in terms which do not seem remote in the twenty-first century:

> KEY QUOTATION
>
> *Thenceforth they press forward on the path of money-getting, losing their esteem for virtue in proportion as the esteem for wealth grows upon them. For can you deny that there is such a gulf between wealth and virtue that, when weighed as it were in the two scales of a balance, one of the two always falls, as the other rises?* (550)

Two fundamental flaws are discerned: first, that the basis for preferment in such a system is wealth, not talent or virtue, and the second that:

> QUOTATION
>
> *such a city must inevitably... become two cities, one comprising the rich, and the other the poor; who reside together on the same ground and are always plotting against each other.* (551)

The profit motive, which is also the 'appetitive' element of the soul which we saw in Chapter 5, comes to govern everything. Like an oriental despot, this appetitive element lords it over the reasoning and spirited elements, forbidding them:

QUOTATION

... to investigate or reason about anything, save how to multiply riches [or] to admire or esteem anything save wealth and the wealthy, or to be ambitious after a single object save the acquisition of riches, and whatever else may conduce to this. (553)

In this powerful denunciation of the all-governing profit motive, we seem very close to certain contemporary critiques by Noam Chomsky, George Monbiot, Naomi Klein, and others of Western democracies as covert oligarchies run by corporations – the notion of the corporate take-over of large parts of the state including government departments and the education system.

DEMOCRACY

Democracy was the characteristic form of government, involving direct participation in decision-making by adult male citizens, of Athens, home to Socrates and Plato. We know by now that Plato had no high opinion of the much-vaunted Athenian democracy – the political system under which his teacher and exemplar as human being and philosopher was put to death. But despite placing democracy as the next-but-worst system of government, Socrates and Plato concede its unrivalled attractiveness. Democracy arises when the poor win power, killing or exiling their opponents. Its great characteristic is freedom:

KEY QUOTATION

Are not [democratic men] free, and does not liberty of act and speech abound in the city, and has not a man licence therein to do what he will? [Democracy is] *an agreeable, lawless, particolored commonwealth, dealing with all alike on a footing of equality, whether they be really equal or not.* (558)

This 'beautiful' kind of polity, which would be most people's choice if they could buy constitutions in a bazaar, obviously, for Socrates and Plato, has grave drawbacks. Democracy, characterized by liberty and diversity, encourages the indulgence of 'useless' desires. Democratic characters (presumably by definition there must quite a variety of democratic characters!) live for the pleasures of the moment: there is no long-term thinking. Here, looking for instance at the failure of Western democracies to implement policies to protect the environment and lessen the impact of climate change, we must acknowledge the acuity of Socrates and Plato's criticisms. However, it is striking that Socrates and Plato see no virtue in the play of voices, the polyphony, which is one of democracy's central features. Nor do they see that democracy's flexibility and accountability to public opinion might constitute a safeguard against malignant authoritarian regimes of the kind too often seen in the twentieth century, which become impossible to dislodge except by violence. The excessive emphasis on unity, as Aristotle says in the *Politics*, means that the ideal state envisaged in *The Republic* makes boring music – unison not harmony.

FROM DEMOCRACY TO TYRANNY – THE UNHAPPINESS OF THE TYRANT

However questionable some of the attempts to correlate political systems and character-types, there is no doubt that Plato achieves an unforgettable success in his portrait of the tyrant. Socrates begins by tracing the descent from democracy into tyranny: the excessive freedom of democracy, under which parents kow-tow to children and teachers to pupils, leads to a total lack of restraint and the election of weak leaders. Tyranny arises as a reaction to this: a popular leader springs up; his regime starts mildly, with wooing of the people, but soon becomes bloodthirsty. Wars and purges are necessary to stave off plots against the insecure leader, who surrounds himself with a bodyguard. This scenario has been re-enacted many times in history, especially in the twentieth century, marked by the murderous violence of such tyrannical regimes as those of Hitler, Stalin and Milosevic.

Here the correlation of regime and character-type is convincing: tyrants do seem in the grip of enslaving passions, often leading to madness, which are disastrously projected onto the world around them. All the associates of tyrants are flatterers, and so '*[tyrants] all their life long live friendless, and always either masters or slaves; for a tyrant nature can never taste real freedom and friendship.*' (576) It certainly does seem difficult to envisage a more miserable condition than that of tyranny, at both individual and social level:

> ## QUOTATION
> *Do you expect to find in any other city more weeping and wailing and lamentation and grief?.... And to return to the individual, do you imagine such things to exist in anyone so abundantly as in this tyrannical man, who is maddened by appetites and longings?* (578)

Socrates and his interlocutors appear to have reached the end of the journey which began with a tug on the sleeve in the Piraeus. The cynical nihilism of Thrasymachus has been definitively put to flight: no one seeing the extreme of misery represented by tyranny could argue than injustice pays. As for justice, even if it remains elusive, it has been shown that the way towards it involves that true orientation or therapy of the mind which is called philosophy. However, there is one further, unexpected episode in the thought-adventure of *The Republic*: an episode which concerns the fate of poetry.

The fate of poetry 11

We have already seen Socrates and Plato impose severe, puritanical censorship on the arts, in an educational context, in Book 3. Poetry and art which do not tell the truth about ultimate realities and which encourage the worst elements of the soul and character (by, for example, representations of indulgence in grief and fear of death) are both psychologically and politically harmful. In Book 10 – one of the most notorious and provocative parts of *The Republic* – they go further, offering a theory of art which seems to prove that dramatic and epic poetry and other representational (mimetic) arts are both constitutionally incapable of telling the truth, and bound to foster disharmony in the soul: thus, despite their potent charm, they must be banished from the city.

POETS AS SKILFUL IMITATORS

This argument appears so crude and bald as almost to have been designed as a provocation. Things become more interesting when Socrates moves from painters to the epic and tragic poets (Homer, Hesiod and the great tragedians) who, as we have seen, had unrivalled prestige in Ancient Greece as seers and moral teachers. They make great claims, to have knowledge of '*all things human which bear upon virtue and vice, and... all things divine.*' If this were really the case, surely Homer and the others would have founded schools or constitutions, or been useful practitioners of an art or skill (*techne*) like medicine. In fact, the poets have no such practical achievements to their names: they are not doctors but merely skilful imitators of doctors' talk. Not only that, poets are deceivers: poetic adornments, the beauties of 'metre, rhythm and harmony,' have the power of a magic spell which persuades the poet's audience that the poet has deep knowledge of things of which he or she is only a superficial imitator.

POETRY FEEDING THE WORTHLESS PART OF THE SOUL

Mimetic poetry has a further undesirable quality: it has an innate tendency to depict conflict rather than harmony:

> QUOTATION
>
> *The imitative poet has, in the nature of things, nothing to do with [the] calm temper of soul... his business is with the peevish and changeful temper, because it is easily imitated.* (605)

Thus the poet – even Homer, the greatest poet, for whom Socrates admits 'an affectionate respect' (595) – cannot be admitted into 'a state that would fain enjoy a good constitution, because he excites and feeds and strengthens [the] worthless part of the soul.'

THE POSSIBILITY OF APPEAL AGAINST BANISHMENT

Socrates and Plato have thrown down a gauntlet. The decree of banishment is not an absolute one: an appeal may be made against the decision. Socrates admits 'there is a quarrel of long standing between poetry and philosophy' (607) – a quarrel which he has no wish to exacerbate.

> QUOTATION
>
> *If poetry, whose end is to please, and imitation, can give any reasons to shew that they ought to exist in a well-constituted state, we for our part will gladly welcome them home again.* (607)

DEFENCE OF POETRY

This provocation is one of the most fertile legacies of *The Republic.*
From Aristotle onwards, the great critical minds of the West have
been stimulated by this attack to muster their defence of the truth-
telling and salutary qualities of art. Aristotle in the *Poetics* develops
the idea of a poetic truth which both distinct from and superior to
historical truth. *'Poetry is concerned with universal truths'*, whereas
'history treats of particular facts.' This makes *'poetry more
philosophical and more worthy of serious attention'* than history.
Secondly, far from merely encouraging the lowest elements of the
soul, Aristotle believes tragedy can have a psychologically beneficial
or therapeutic effect, *'by means of pity and fear bringing about the
purgation (catharsis) of such emotions.'* (*Classical Literary Criticism,*
Harmondsworth: Penguin, 1965, p.39)

These arguments have been developed and rephrased repeatedly
down the centuries. The Romantics in particular championed the
idea of poetry and the other arts as creative rather than imitative. In
Shelley's words, poetry *'awakens and enlarges the mind itself by
rendering it the receptacle of a thousand unapprehended combinations
of thought.'* In an age dominated by calculation, poetry unshackles
imagination which according to Shelley is a moral force. The repeated
attempts by totalitarian regimes to control or silence artists seem to
bear witness to a vitally subversive quality in art, an anarchic
principle which could challenge Plato's 'idea of the good'.

THE GREAT PARADOX: PLATO AS POET

The greatest paradox of Book 10 is, of course, that Plato, who
through the figure of Socrates proposes to banish poets from his
ideal state, is himself a poet – according to Shelley, a *'poet of the very
first rank'.* Not only did Plato compose (formal) poetry in his youth,
but time and again, at particularly charged moments in the
dialogues, he resorts to a non-dialectical mode of myth or poetry.
Examples in *The Republic* include the great myth of the Cave, the
metaphor of the sun, the 'noble lie' or myth of the metals – a central

plank of *The Republic*'s political vision – and the concluding myth of Er. Myths embody or express what Julius Elias has called 'indemonstrable axioms' – unprovable key insights which lie at the heart of all systems of thought.

What differentiates the Platonic myths from the kind of misleading poetry he intends to outlaw? First, the Platonic myths are always carefully flagged, and do not claim to be truths, but provisional illustrations of things which cannot be grasped directly (for instance, the nature of the good). Secondly, though their origin may lie in inspiration, or divine madness, they can and must be subjected to scrutiny and evaluation by the power of human reason. Poetry as metaphor is not banished from *The Republic*: what Socrates and Plato will not admit is the kind of bad art which makes unjustifiable claims and has deleterious moral and psychological effects.

EPILOGUE: THE MYTH OF ER

The Republic ends with a myth – a religious myth at that. The story of Er is preceded by Socrates's assertion that the soul is immortal (an assertion which takes Glaucon by surprise), which he justifies on the grounds that nothing can be destroyed except by its own particular 'evil': as the soul's particular evil is wickedness, which destroys others but not the self, the soul must be indestructible.

The story of Er, based on the Pythagorean doctrine of the transmigration of souls, takes us definitively away from the political realm and into that of ethics and religion, from this world to 'the other world'. Er is a soldier killed in battle who is chosen as a messenger to report back to the human world what happens when souls are judged and then when the dead are allowed to choose a new life. Wrong-doers are made '*to undergo tenfold sufferings for all and each of their offences*' (615) while the virtuous are correspondingly rewarded. When it comes to the choice of a new life, the unenlightened majority simply repeat the conventional errors of past lives (here we might think of the Freudian theory of 'repetition compulsion'). Despite this, it is possible for an enlightened, philosophising soul to '*discriminate between a good and an evil life*' (618) and choose wisely. Such a one is represented by Odysseus, who after all his sufferings opts for the lot (rejected by others) of an ordinary man. The myth of Er is Plato's final, religious assertion of the superiority of justice to injustice and of the examined, philosophical life to the unexamined.

GLOSSARY OF MAIN GREEK WORDS

aporia, difficulty, perplexity

dikaios, just, good, upright

dikaiosyne, justice, goodness, uprightness

doxa, opinion, belief

elenchus, the Socratic method of questioning and refutation

episteme, true knowledge, understanding

epithumetikon, to, the desiring, appetitive part of the mind

logistikon, to, the reasoning part of the mind

philosophia, love of wisdom, philosophy

phylax, guard, guardian

polis, city, state, society

politeia, citizenship, government, constitution, republic

psyche, mind, soul

soma, body

techne, art, skill

thumos, spiritedness, moral indignation

GUIDE TO THINKERS MENTIONED IN THE TEXT

Aristotle (384–22 BC) Greek philosopher, pupil of Plato. Author of works on logic, metaphysics, ethics, politics, drama and biology.

Augustine of Hippo, Saint (354–430) Father of the Christian Church, whose *The City of* God is inspired by an ethico-religious reading of Plato's *The Republic.*

Bacon, Francis (1561–1626) English politician and philosopher. His *Novum Organum* inaugurates the theory of scientific method.

Chomsky, Noam (1928–) American linguist and political thinker.

Derrida, Jacques (1930–) Algerian-French-Jewish philosopher, founder of Deconstructionism.

Donne, John (1572–1631) English poet and clergyman.

Jung, Carl (1875–1961) Swiss psychoanalyst. Initially a disciple of Freud, he developed his own theories of archetypes and the collective unconscious.

Kant, Immanuel (1724–1804) German philosopher, whose distinction between appearances (*phenomena*) and things-as-they-are (*noumena*) harks back to Plato.

Kierkegaard, Søren (1813–55) Danish religious philosopher, precursor of existentialism. Author of *On the Concept of Irony with Constant Reference to Socrates.*

Klein, Melanie (1882–1966) British psychoanalyst, noted for her work on early infancy.

Mill, John Stuart (1806–73) English philosopher. *On Liberty* defends the freedoms of individuals and minorities against tyrannical majorities and public opinion.

Miller, Alice (1923–) Psychoanalyst, author of *Drama of Being a Child* (first published as *Drama of the Gifted Child*), which highlights the difficulties of especially gifted children.

Milton, John (1608–74) English poet and controversialist. *Areopagitica* is a public oration defending freedom of the press.

Monbiot, George (1963–) British ecologist and political thinker. His *Captive State* analyses the infiltration of corporate influence into all areas of the UK body politic.

Montaigne, Michel de (1533–92) French philosopher, whose sceptical and humane *Essays* show the influence of Socrates.

Nietzsche, Friedrich (1844–1900) Great and controversial German philosopher. *The Birth of Tragedy* accuses Socratic and Platonic reason of destroying the spirit of tragedy.

Pascal, Blaise (1623–62) French philosopher and mathematician, author of *Pensees*. 'Pascal's wager' is an argument for the rationality of belief in God.

Rousseau, Jean-Jacques (1712–78) Swiss political and education philosopher, whose *Social Contract* influenced the leaders of t French Revolution.

Shelley, Percy Bysshe (1792–1822) English Romantic poet. I prose work *A Defence of Poetry* responds to *Republic* Book10.

Xenophon (c. 430–355 BC) Greek writer and historian, friend a admirer of Socrates, whom he recalls in *Memorabilia*.

FURTHER READING

Annas, Julia, *Introduction to Plato's Republic* (Oxford: OUP, 1982): the best full-length guide to *The Republic.*

Aristotle, *Politics* (tr. Benjamin Jowett, Oxford: OUP, 1905): the first great response to Plato's *Republic.*

Crossman, Richard, *Plato Today* (London: Allen and Unwin, 1959): though less topical than when originally written in 1937, this is still a lively discussion of Plato's political and educational ideas.

Cushman, Robert, *Therapeia* (Chapel Hill: University of North Carolina Press, 1958): an eloquent, existentially informed reading of Plato's philosophy, focusing on its ethical drive.

Elias, Julius, *Plato's Defence of Poetry* (London: Macmillan, 1984): a good corrective to Karl Popper's partial view.

Huxley, Aldous, *Brave New World* (London: Chatto & Windus, 1932): the famous dystopian satire of the future partly inspired by *The Republic* Book 5.

More, Sir Thomas, *Utopia*: an essay about a 'nowhere-land' whose good government includes education for men and women and religious toleration, inspired by *The Republic.*

Murdoch, Iris, *Metaphysics as a Guide to Morals* (London: Chatto & Windus, 1992): a vast philosophical compendium, with illuminating sections on Plato and *The Republic.*

Murdoch, Iris, *The Fire and the Sun* (Oxford: OUP, 1977): a sympathetic reading of Plato's banishing of the artists.

Nehamas, Alexander, *The Art of Living* (Berkeley: University of California Press, 1998): a fascinating account of Socratic and Platonic irony and the influence of Socrates on Montaigne, Nietzsche and Foucault.

Popper, Karl, *The Open Society and Its Enemies, Vol. 1* (London: Routledge, 1966): a powerful and influential polemic, which brands Plato as a totalitarian, missing some of his irony.

INDEX